A NAV

M000202612

*A life-changing
encounter with God's Word*

1 & 2
CHRONICLES

*Move beyond forgetfulness to see
God's faithfulness in your own life.*

NavPress

A NavPress resource published in alliance
with Tyndale House Publishers, Inc.

NavPress is the publishing ministry of The Navigators, an international Christian organization and leader in personal spiritual development. NavPress is committed to helping people grow spiritually and enjoy lives of meaning and hope through personal and group resources that are biblically rooted, culturally relevant, and highly practical.

For more information, visit www.NavPress.com.

1 and 2 Chronicles

A NavPress resource published in alliance with Tyndale House Publishers, Inc.

NAVPRESS is a registered trademark of NavPress, The Navigators, Colorado Springs, CO. The NAVPRESS logo is a trademark of NavPress, The Navigators. *TYNDALE* is a registered trademark of Tyndale House Publishers, Inc. Absence of ® in connection with marks of NavPress or other parties does not indicate an absence of registration of those marks.

For information about special discounts for bulk purchases, please contact Tyndale House Publishers at csresponse@tyndale.com, or call 1-800-323-9400.

ISBN 978-1-61521-766-3

Printed in the United States of America

24	23	22	21	20	19	18
8	7	6	5	4	3	2

CONTENTS

How to Use This Guide   5

Introduction — The Books of 1 and 2 Chronicles: A Chosen Nation,
a Privileged Mission   11

One — The Heritage of God's People (1 Chronicles 1–7)   15

Two — The Rise of David (1 Chronicles 8–12)   25

Three — The Reign of David (1 Chronicles 13–20)   33

Four — David's Later Days (1 Chronicles 21–27)   43

Five — The Rise of Solomon (1 Chronicles 28–29; 2 Chronicles 1–5)   53

Six — The Reign of Solomon (2 Chronicles 6–9)   63

Seven — The Kingdom Divided (2 Chronicles 10–16)   71

Eight — The Reign of Jehoshaphat (2 Chronicles 17–20)   83

Nine — Further Crises (2 Chronicles 21–24)   91

Ten — Further Decline (2 Chronicles 25–28)   99

Eleven — The Reign of Hezekiah (2 Chronicles 29–32)   107

Twelve — The Kingdom's Fall (2 Chronicles 33–36)   117

Study Aids   129

HOW TO USE THIS GUIDE

Although the LifeChange guides vary with the individual books they explore, they share some common goals:

1. To provide you with a firm foundation of understanding, plus a thirst to return to the book throughout your life.

2. To give you study patterns and skills that help you explore every part of the Bible.

3. To offer you historical background, word definitions, and explanation notes to aid your study.

4. To help you grasp the message of the book as a whole.

5. To teach you how to let God's Word transform you into Christ's image.

As you begin

This guide includes twelve lessons that will take you chapter by chapter through all of 1 and 2 Chronicles. To benefit most from this time, here's a good way to begin your work on each lesson:

1. Pray for God's help to keep you mentally alert and spiritually sensitive.

2. Read attentively the entire passage mentioned in the lesson's title. (You may want to read the passage from two or more Bible versions — perhaps at least once from a more literal translation such as the New International Version, English Standard Version, New American Standard Bible, or New King James Version and perhaps once more in a paraphrase such as *The Message* or the New Living Translation.) Do your reading in an environment that's as free as possible from distractions. Allow your mind and heart to meditate on the words you encounter — words that are God's personal gift to you and to all His people.

After reading the passage, you're ready to dive into the numbered questions in this guide that make up the main portion of each lesson. Each of these questions is followed by blank space for writing your answers. (This act of writing your answers helps clarify your thinking and stimulates your mental engagement with the passage as well as your later recall.) Use extra paper or a notebook if the space for recording your answers seems too cramped. Continue through the questions in numbered order. If any question seems too difficult or unclear, just skip it and go on to the next.

Most of the questions will direct you back to 1 and 2 Chronicles to look again at a certain portion of the assigned passage for that lesson. At this point, be sure to use a more literal Bible translation rather than a paraphrase.

As you look closer at a passage, it's helpful to approach it in this progression:

Observe. What does the passage actually *say*? Ask God to help you see it clearly. Notice everything that's there.

Interpret. What does the passage *mean*? Ask God to help you understand. And remember that any passage's meaning is fundamentally determined by its *context.* So stay alert to all you see about the setting and background of 1 and 2 Chronicles, and keep thinking of each book as a whole while you proceed through it chapter by chapter. You'll be progressively building up your insights and familiarity with what it's all about.

Apply. Keep asking yourself, *How does this truth affect my life?* Pray for God's help as you examine yourself in light of that truth and in light of His purpose for each passage.

Try to consciously follow all three of these steps as you shape your written answer to each question in the lesson.

The extras

In addition to the regular numbered questions you see in this guide, each lesson also offers several "optional" questions or suggestions that appear in the margins. All of these will appear under one of three headings:

Optional Application. These are suggested options for application. Consider these with prayerful sensitivity to the Lord's guidance.

For Thought and Discussion. Many of these questions address various ethical issues and other biblical principles that lead to a wide range of implications. They tend to be particularly suited for group discussion.

For Further Study. These often include cross-references to other parts of the Bible that shed light on a topic in the lesson, plus questions that delve deeper into the passage.

(For additional help for more effective Bible study, refer to the "Study Aids" section starting on page 129.)

Changing your life

Don't let your study become an exercise in knowledge alone. Treat the passage as God's Word, and stay in dialogue with Him as you study. Pray, "Lord, what do You want me to notice here?" "Father, why is this true?" "Lord, how does my life measure up to this?" Let biblical truth sink into your inner convictions so you'll increasingly be able to act on this truth as a natural way of living.

At times you may want to consider memorizing a certain verse or passage you come across in your study, one that particularly challenges or encourages you. To help with that, write down the words on a card to keep with you, and set aside a few minutes each day to think about the passage. Recite it to yourself repeatedly, always thinking about its meaning. Return to it as often as you can for a brief review. You'll soon find the words coming to mind spontaneously, and they'll begin to affect your motives and actions.

For group study

Exploring Scripture together in a group is especially valuable for the encouragement, support, and accountability it provides as you seek to apply God's Word to your life. Together you can listen jointly for God's guidance, pray for each other, help one another resist temptation, and share the spiritual principles you're learning to put into practice. Together you affirm that growing in faith, hope, and love is important and that you need each other in the process.

A group of four to ten people allows for the closest understanding of each other and the richest discussions in Bible study, but you can adapt this guide for other-sized groups. It will suit a wide range of group types, such as home Bible studies, growth groups, youth groups, and church classes. Both new and mature Christians will benefit from the guide, regardless of their previous experience in Bible study.

Aim for a positive atmosphere of acceptance, honesty, and openness. In your first meeting, explore candidly everyone's expectations and goals for your time together.

A typical schedule for group study is to take one lesson per week, but feel free to split lessons if you want to discuss them more thoroughly. Or omit some questions in a lesson if your preparation or discussion time is limited. (You can always return to this guide later for further study on your own.)

When you come together, you probably won't have time to discuss all the questions in the lesson, so it's helpful to choose ahead of time the ones you want to make sure to cover thoroughly. This is one of the main responsibilities a group leader typically assumes.

Each lesson in this guide ends with a section called "For the group." It gives advice for that particular lesson on how to focus the discussion, how to apply the lesson to daily life, and so on. Reading each lesson's "For the group" section ahead of time can help the leader be more effective in guiding the group.

You'll get the greatest benefit from your time together if each group member also prepares ahead of time by writing out his or her answers to each question in the lesson. The private reflection and prayer this preparation can stimulate will be especially important in helping everyone discern how God wants you to apply each lesson to your daily lives.

There are many ways to structure the group meeting, and in fact you may want to vary your routine occasionally to help keep things fresh.

Here are some of the elements you can consider including as you come together for each lesson:

Pray together. It's good to pause for prayer as you begin your time together. When you begin with prayer, it's worthwhile and honoring to God to ask especially for His Holy Spirit's guidance of your time together. If you write down each other's prayer requests, you are more likely to remember to pray for them during the week, ask about them at the next meeting, and notice answered prayers. You might want to get a notebook for prayer requests and discussion notes

Worship. Some groups like to sing together and worship God with prayers of praise.

Review. You may want to take time to discuss what difference the previous week's lesson has made in your lives as well as recall the major emphasis you discovered in the passage for that week.

Read the passage aloud. Once you're ready to focus attention together on the assigned Scripture passage in the week's lesson, read it aloud. (One person could do this, or the reading could be shared.)

Open up for questions. Allow time for group members to mention anything in the passage they may have particular questions about.

Summarize the passage. Have one or two people offer a summary of what the passage says.

Discuss. This will be the heart of your time together and will likely take the biggest portion of your time. Focus on the questions you see as the most important and most helpful. Allow and encourage everyone to be part of the discussion for each question. You may want to take written notes as the discussion proceeds. Ask follow-up questions to sharpen your attention and deepen your understanding of what you discuss. You may want to give special attention to the questions in the margins under the heading "For Thought and Discussion."

Encourage further personal study. You can find more opportunities for exploring this lesson's themes and issues under the heading "For Further Study" in the margins throughout the lesson. You can also pursue some of these together during your group time.

Focus on application. Look especially at the "Optional Application" listed in the margins throughout the lesson. Keep encouraging one another in the continual work of adjusting your lives to the truths God gives in Scripture.

Summarize your discoveries. You may want to read aloud through the passage one last time together, using the opportunity to solidify your understanding and appreciation of it and clarify how the Lord is speaking to you through it.

Look ahead. Glance together at the headings and questions in the next lesson to see what's coming next.

Give thanks to God. It's good to end your time together by pausing to express gratitude to God for His Word and the work of His Spirit in your minds and hearts during your time together.

Keep these worthy guidelines in mind throughout your time together:

Let us consider how we may spur one another on toward love and good deeds.

(HEBREWS 10:24)

Carry each other's burdens, and in this way you will fulfill the law of Christ.

(GALATIANS 6:2)

Accept one another, then, just as Christ accepted you, in order to bring praise to God.

(ROMANS 15:7)

THE BOOKS OF 1 AND 2 CHRONICLES

A Chosen Nation, a Privileged Mission

What do you do when life isn't turning out the way you expected it would? What if there seems to be a disconnect between the life the Bible promises and the life you actually have? You're struggling with confusion and disappointment, and trying to hold onto faith. This is the situation the books of 1 and 2 Chronicles were written to address.

A disappointed nation

In 450-400 BC, a fragile community of Jews lives in the southern part of the Promised Land. Judah isn't a free nation but an insignificant backwater ruled by the Persian Empire. The Jews have a temple in Jerusalem, but it is a poor shadow of the magnificent temple that stood there for centuries before the Babylonians turned it to rubble. That catastrophe is 150 years in the past now, a distant legend, but the Jews are still trying to make sense of it.

The prophets wrote that after God let the Babylonians destroy Jerusalem and take the Jews into exile, He would restore Israel to its former glory. Yet the great-grandparents of today's Jews returned from exile a hundred years ago, and it would be laughable to call their little nation glorious. Harvests are sometimes terrible. Persia demands taxes to fund its wars with Greece. Those two superpowers have impressive, well-funded religions that overshadow Judah's worship of her God. Just north of Judah, the Samaritans practice an odious religion that mixes the old faith of Israel with paganism. And to cap it all off, the Jews themselves are constantly squabbling with one another.

They wonder, where is God? Is He greater than the gods of the superpowers? Are the Jews truly heirs to God's promises? How should they worship? Is there any hope of a king descended from the great King David?

A pastor's heart

An educated Jew, a member of the priestly tribe of Levi, and possibly a priest himself, has a pastor's heart to respond to such questions. He is steeped in the Bible from Genesis through Kings, and he sees God's hand in the whole history of his people. This pastor wants them to step back from their day-to-day frustrations and see the big story they are part of. We don't know his name; we call him simply "the Chronicler." He writes an account of God and His people from Adam to the exile, to help the people of his generation understand who God is and what He is up to.

His main source is the earlier books of the Bible, although he may use other sources that haven't survived. As history, Chronicles is a supplement to the other books, especially 1 and 2 Samuel and 1 and 2 Kings.

Overview of Chronicles

In Hebrew, Chronicles is one book. It was divided in two when it was translated into Greek a few centuries before Christ. An outline looks like this:

I. 1 Chronicles 1–9. Genealogies trace the family of God's promise from Adam to Abraham, to Judah, to David, to the royal line after David, followed by the other tribes of Israel including Levi (the Chronicler's tribe). Genealogies then identify the Jews who returned to Judah after the exile (the recent ancestors of those living when the Chronicler wrote).
II. 1 Chronicles 10–29. King David is the ideal king who establishes Israel, fights off Israel's enemies, and prepares for the building of the temple.
III. 2 Chronicles 1–9. King Solomon follows David's pattern by building the temple and ruling a kingdom of peace and prosperity.
IV. 2 Chronicles 10–36. The kingdom splits apart after Solomon's death, the kings of Judah plunge into sin, and God has to judge them. Chronicles ends with the exile to Babylon and a brief mention of Persia letting the Jews return to their homeland after the exile.

Message and themes

The themes the Chronicler addresses include:

- God has a covenant relationship with His people—what does that mean and why does it matter?
- We worship a generous God who chose one nation in order to bless all nations.
- God exiled His people from the Promised Land because of sin but restored them to the land because of His grace and their repentance.
- God reveals His nature in how He acts in the details of history.

- Worship is crucial.
- Obedience to God's Word is crucial.
- Sin brings disaster and judgment from God.
- God never stops offering grace.
- God is sovereign over His people's lives and history.
- The present is connected to the past. The past matters now.
- The future is full of hope.
- God's people are one.

1 CHRONICLES 1–7

The Heritage of God's People

1. For getting the most from 1 and 2 Chronicles, one of the best guidelines is found in 2 Timothy 3:16-17, words Paul wrote with the Old Testament first in view. He said that *all* Scripture is of great benefit to (a) teach us, (b) rebuke us, (c) correct us, and (d) train us in righteousness. Paul added that these Scriptures completely equip the person of God "for every good work." As you think seriously about those guidelines, in which of these areas do you especially want to experience the usefulness of 1 and 2 Chronicles? Express your desire in a written prayer to God.

_____

_____

_____

_____

_____

2. In Jeremiah 23:29, God says that His Word is "like fire" and "like a hammer." He can use the Scriptures to burn away unclean thoughts

Optional Application: We read that after Jesus' resurrection, when He was explaining Old Testament passages to His disciples, He "opened their minds so they could understand the Scriptures" (Luke 24:45). Ask God to do that kind of work in *your* mind as you study 1 and 2 Chronicles so you're released and free to learn everything He wants you to learn here and so you can become as bold, worshipful, and faithful as those early disciples of Jesus were. Express this desire to Him in prayer.

For Thought and Discussion: Before launching into a closer look at 1 and 2 Chronicles, summarize what you already know about these books.

and desires in our hearts. He can also use Scripture, with hammer-like hardness, to crush and crumble our spiritual hardness. From your study of 1 and 2 Chronicles, how do you most want to see the fire-and-hammer power of God's Word at work in your own life? Again, express this longing in a written prayer to God.

_____

_____

_____

_____

_____

_____

3. Think about these words of Paul to his younger helper Timothy: "Do your best to present yourself to God as one approved, a worker who does not need to be ashamed and who correctly handles the word of truth" (2 Timothy 2:15). God calls you to be a "worker" as you study God's word of truth in 1 and 2 Chronicles. It takes *work*—concentration and perseverance—to fully appropriate God's blessings for us in these books. Express here your commitment before God to work diligently in this study of Chronicles.

_____

_____

_____

_____

_____

4. In one sitting if possible, read attentively all of 1 Chronicles 1–7, taking notes and underlining or highlighting as you go. What impresses you overall as the key features and themes of this part of the book?

_____

_____

_____

_____

The point of the genealogies in chapters 1–9 is to show that the Jews living in the Chronicler's generation are the legitimate heirs of the promise that can be traced from Adam, to Abraham, to Judah and the other patriarchs, to King David. The genealogies sometimes skip generations, sometimes deal with several family lines at once (see 6:1-3), sometimes drop in a story about some event (see 4:9-10; 5:18-22). They deal with all twelve tribes of Israel, but the focus is on the royal family of David and the priestly tribe of Levi. Those two families lead in the secular and the sacred realms.

Genealogies may bore us, but they show how deeply the Jews valued family and how important family was at a time when God's promises passed through bloodlines. Each individual, even if he is only a name on a page to us, is a whole valued piece of the story to God. History, too, matters to God. Our faith is not merely a list of doctrinal propositions. It is rooted in events that happened in particular times and places to particular people.

5. "The opening chapter, drawn almost wholly from Genesis, traces the descent of Israel (Jacob) from Adam and depicts the place of his

descendants among the nations."[1] In this first chapter of 1 Chronicles, which of the persons listed are familiar to you from other parts of Scripture?

_____

_____

_____

Adam (1:1). The story of God's covenant of promise begins where human history begins.

Abraham (1:28). Abraham is the center point between Adam (see 1:1) and Jacob/Israel (see 2:1). All of Abraham's descendants are named to show that God kept His promise to make Abraham the father of many nations (see Genesis 17:3-6).[2]

---

6. In chapters 2–4, the genealogies focus on the tribe of Judah, with special emphasis on the family of David (in chapters 3 and 4). In addition to David, which of the persons listed in chapters 2–4 are familiar to you from other parts of Scripture?

_____

_____

_____

The sons of Israel (2:1). All twelve tribes are listed in 2:1-2. For the Chronicler, the restoration of Israel will be complete only when all twelve tribes are restored to the land. It's not enough to restore Judah.

The sons of Judah (2:3). Faithful leadership was supposed to come through the tribe of Judah. Her failure to provide that leadership led to the exile, but God isn't finished with Judah. She still has a central role in God's plan.

These were the sons of David (3:1). God promised
that the family of David would be the royal line
of His people forever (see 1 Chronicles 14:2;
2 Chronicles 2:11). This family is key to God's
plan.

In chapter 3, the Chronicler lists the
kings from David's line and then the
descendants of David who survived the
exile. The promised royal line will have to
pass through one of those descendants.
Ultimately, the Messiah will descend from
one of these, so these are important
names. They include the two men who
led the first and second waves of exiles
back to the Promised Land.

7. What theological significance and spiritual
instruction do you see in the brief story of Jabez
in 4:9-10?

_____

_____

_____

_____

***Jabez cried out to the God of Israel . . . and God
granted his request*** (4:10). The Chronicler
often notes that prayer to the God of Israel is
answered (see 1 Chronicles 5:20-22; 2 Chronicles 20:6-12). He wants his readers to pray.

8. In focusing on the genealogy of Israel's
Transjordan tribes, chapter 5 emphasizes tribes
that were exiled by the Assyrians a century
before Babylon destroyed Judah (see 5:6,22,26).

Which of the persons listed here are familiar to you from other parts of Scripture?

_____

_____

_____

A ruler came from [Judah] (5:2). King David.

The battle was God's (5:22). The Chronicler's faith about warfare is that God helps His people win battles and that their prayers are crucial (see 1 Chronicles 12:19; 15:26; 2 Chronicles 20:15; 25:8; 32:10).[3]

9. What theological significance and spiritual instruction do you see in how the historical record is presented in 5:24-26?

_____

_____

_____

10. In chapter 6, the genealogy focuses on the tribe of Levi. Which of the persons listed here are familiar to you from other parts of Scripture?

_____

_____

11. What responsibilities and duties of the Levites are mentioned in chapter 6?

_____

_____

_____

The sons of Levi (6:1). The Levites get lengthy treatment because they led the nation's worship and the Chronicler placed a high value on worship. Many interpreters think he was a Levite himself. His readers would have known some of the names—Moses, Aaron, Miriam, Nadab, Abihu, and more—from other stories in the Bible. The mention of these names would have reminded his readers to learn from these people's virtues and sins.

The men David put in charge of the music in the house of the LORD (6:31). The Chronicler gives much attention to music in worship, and the men who led it. See 1 Chronicles 6:31-47; 9:33; 15:16-24; 23:5; 25:1-31; 2 Chronicles 5:12-13; 7:6; 29:25-30; 34:12.

Heman (6:33). A music ministry leader from the time of David (see 6:31; 15:16-19). He played the bronze cymbals when the ark of the covenant was brought into Jerusalem (see 15:19) and at other times (see 16:42). The superscription of Psalm 88 says Heman wrote it.

Asaph (6:39). Asaph too played the cymbals in David's day (see 15:19). The guild of Asaph wrote a dozen psalms (Psalms 50; 73–83), including the psalm for the ark's entrance into Jerusalem (see 1 Chronicles 16:7).

Ethan (6:44). Another cymbal player (see 15:19). The superscription of Psalm 89 says he wrote it.

Making atonement for Israel (6:49). The priests were Levites from the line of Aaron, and this was their most important task. "The word 'atonement' essentially means 'to cover.' God ordained that sin be 'covered' by means of animal sacrifice, whether offered for individuals (as in Leviticus 4:29,31) or the entire nation of Israel on the Day of Atonement (see Leviticus 16). The sacrificial offerings were symbolic of atonement since 'it is impossible for the blood of bulls and goats to take away sin' (Hebrews 10:4)."[4]

For Further Study: What more can you learn about the duties of the Levites (see 1 Chronicles 6) from Numbers 3:6-9 and 18:5? (See also 1 Chronicles 23:28-31.)

12. In chapter 7, the genealogy focuses on the northern tribes of Issachar, Benjamin, Naphtali, Manasseh, Ephraim, and Asher. Which of the persons listed here are familiar to you from other parts of Scripture?

_____

_____

_____

13. What would you say is the main point being made in chapter 7 by including the incident described in 7:21-24?

_____

_____

_____

_____

The story of Ezer and Elead in 7:21-24 does not come from elsewhere in the Bible. The Chronicler adds it to exhort his readers that a temporary loss can be overcome by God's grace and human action. Likewise, the great loss of the exile was temporary and is being overcome.[5]

14. Imagine that you were an Israelite living in Judah after the return from Babylonian exile. What overall impressions and lessons of your national and spiritual heritage would you gain from these genealogical chapters at the beginning of 1 Chronicles?

_____

_____

_____

_____

15. In 1 Chronicles 1–7, what would you select as the key verse or passage—one that best captures or reflects the dynamics of what these chapters are all about?

_____

_____

_____

_____

16. List any lingering questions you have about 1 Chronicles 1–7.

_____

_____

_____

_____

Optional Application: On the basis of God's truth revealed to you in this lesson, perhaps the Holy Spirit has helped you sense a new and higher reality in your life that God is inviting you to. If this is true for you, express in your own words the reality that you long for, and use it as a springboard for prayer.

For the group

In your first meeting, it may be helpful to turn to the front of this book and review together the "How to Use This Guide" section.

You may want to focus your discussion for lesson 1 especially on some of the following issues, themes, and concepts (which are recognized as major overall themes in 1 and 2 Chronicles). Which of these are dealt with in some way in chapters 1–7, and how are they further developed there?

- The meaning and significance of God's covenant relationship with His people
- God's nature, especially as revealed by how He acts in the details of His people's history
- The importance and meaning of worship
- For God's people, the continuity of the present with the past
- The importance of obedience to God's Word and His laws, and our personal responsibility in that regard
- How sin brings disaster and judgment from God
- God's continued blessings and grace for His people

- The future hope of God's people
- The unity of God's people
- God's sovereignty over His people's lives and history

The following numbered questions in lesson 1 may stimulate your best and most helpful discussion: 4, 7, 9, 13, 14, 15, and 16.

Look also at the exercise in the margin under the heading "For Thought and Discussion."

1. *ESV Study Bible* (Wheaton, IL: Crossway, 2008), at 1 Chronicles 1:1–9:44.
2. Andrew E. Hill, *1 & 2 Chronicles*, The NIV Application Commentary series, ed. Terry Much (Grand Rapids, MI: Zondervan, 2003), 63.
3. Hill, 120.
4. Hill, 138–139.
5. Hill, 154.

1 CHRONICLES 8–12

The Rise of David

1. In one sitting if possible, read attentively all of
1 Chronicles 8–12, taking notes and underlining or highlighting as you go. What impresses
you overall as the key features and themes of
this part of the book?

_____

_____

_____

_____

2. In chapter 8, the genealogy focuses on the tribe
of Benjamin (Saul's tribe). Besides Saul, which
of the persons listed here are familiar to you
from other parts of Scripture?

_____

_____

_____

The genealogy of Benjamin in chapter 8
introduces the genealogy of King Saul in
9:35-44. Saul was Israel's first king, David's
predecessor, and an example of failed

25

kingship. Later, when Israel split into two kingdoms, Israel and Judah, Benjamin became part of the kingdom of Judah. In the Chronicler's day, Benjamin was part of the province of Judah. Benjamin and Judah were thus the two tribes that were carrying on the faith and social identity of God's people, while the other tribes were still largely scattered.

Esh-Baal (8:33). Ishvi in 1 Samuel 14:49 and Ish-Bosheth in 2 Samuel 4:1.

Merib-Baal (8:34). Mephibosheth in 2 Samuel 4:4.

In chapter 9 the Chronicler suddenly jumps ahead to the people who resettled Judah after the exile in Babylon. They are the culmination of all these genealogies, the heirs of God's promises who were faithful enough to face the difficulties of traveling back and rebuilding Judah.

All Israel (9:1). The Chronicler uses this phrase often. It refers to the heirs of God's promises.[1] The Chronicler wants his readers to think in terms of the whole people of God as one people, not the two kingdoms of Israel and Judah that for so long were at each other's throats.[2]

In Jerusalem (9:3). The prophets' promises for rebuilding Israel center on Jerusalem (see Isaiah 44:26,28; Jeremiah 33:16), so the holy city looms large in the Chronicler's vision. By resettling Jerusalem, these individuals were beginning to fulfill the promises.

---

3. How would you summarize the importance for God's people of the information given in chapter 9?

_____

_____

_____

4. In 9:35-44, why do you think Saul's family record is repeated here from the previous chapter?

_____

_____

_____

_____

5. In chapter 10, what does the author of Chronicles (and the Holy Spirit) appear to emphasize most about Saul in this account of how he died?

_____

_____

_____

_____

At 10:1, the Chronicler shifts suddenly from genealogy to narrative. He deals with Saul chiefly as an introduction to the story that really interests him: the story of David, heir of God's promise.

6. What does chapter 10 demonstrate about retribution for sin?

_____

_____

_____

_____

For Further Study:
Compare 1 Chronicles 9 to the similar account in Nehemiah 11.

For Thought and Discussion:
The resettling of Jerusalem after the Babylonian captivity (as described in 1 Chronicles 9) does not take place until long after the other events recorded in both 1 and 2 Chronicles. Why then do you think the Chronicler chose to place this information at this point in the book instead of at the end of 2 Chronicles?

For Further Study:
Compare 1 Chronicles
10:1-14 to the parallel
account in 1 Samuel
31 and 2 Samuel 1.

7. What theological significance and spiritual
instruction do you see in the words about Saul
in 10:13-14?

_____

_____

_____

_____

_____

Saul . . . was unfaithful (10:13). Saul failed in key
ways: he was unfaithful, he was disobedient,
he consulted a medium, and he didn't ask for
guidance from the Lord. In Chronicles, these
traits often lead to God's judgment (see also
2 Chronicles 12:2; 26:16; 28:19). Saul is an individual example of the sins that led to the exile.

The LORD put him to death (10:14). The Philistines
who fought Saul were instruments of God's
judgment, just as the Babylonians were God's
instruments at the time of the exile. God is
always in charge.

8. In chapter 11, what are the most important
factors and perspectives regarding David's rise
to the throne?

_____

_____

_____

_____

Hebron (11:1). Centuries earlier, Abraham and
Sarah, Isaac and Rebekah, and Jacob and Leah
all lived and were buried here.

9. In 11:1-2, what is particularly significant in the statements made by the people about David?

_____

_____

_____

_____

For Further Study: Compare 1 Chronicles 11:1-9 to the parallel account in 2 Samuel 5:1-10.

For Thought and Discussion: What impresses you most in the descriptions of David's "mighty warriors" in 11:10-47?

For Further Study: Compare 1 Chronicles 11:10-47 to the parallel account in 2 Samuel 23:8-39.

The Lord Almighty was with him (11:9). David's faithfulness and obedience are "the standard by which his successors will be measured."[3]

The chiefs of David's mighty warriors . . . the Three . . . the Thirty (11:10,18,25). The Thirty are an elite unit of "mighty warriors" — professional soldiers who live and die by loyalty to God and king. The Three are the commanders of that unit. Their loyalty and bravery are examples for the Chronicler's readers to follow. His generation needs that kind of united support for the good leaders whom the Chronicler hopes God will send.[4]

The Lord brought about a great victory (11:14). The Chronicler believes his nation's security depends not on the valor of mighty warriors but on a mighty God.

They risked their lives (11:19). A leadership quality that the Chronicler highlights is David's ability to "inspire remarkable bravery and unshakable loyalty."[5]

10. What conclusions can you make from chapter 12 about David's leadership and about the loyalty and skill of the warriors he led?

_____

_____

_____

_____

Optional Application: What notable leadership principles do you see on display in chapter 12 that relate to your own areas of leadership responsibility?

11. What action on the part of God's Spirit do you see in 12:18, and what does this passage teach us about how the Spirit works?

_____

_____

_____

_____

12. What principles for spiritual warfare do you see illustrated in chapter 12?

_____

_____

_____

_____

These were the men who came to David (12:1). Armed men who followed David when he was king over just Judah, before he became king over all Israel. This chapter thus takes place chronologically before chapter 11.

---

13. What timeless spiritual principles do you see emphasized in the details of Israel's history as recorded in 1 Chronicles 8–12?

_____

_____

_____

_____

14. How would you summarize the most important perspectives these chapters give us about the man David?

_____

_____

_____

_____

15. In 1 Chronicles 8–12, what would you select as the key verse or passage — one that best captures or reflects the dynamics of what these chapters are all about?

_____

_____

_____

_____

16. List any lingering questions you have about 1 Chronicles 8–12.

_____

_____

_____

_____

Optional Application: On the basis of God's truth revealed to you in this lesson, perhaps the Holy Spirit has helped you sense a new and higher reality in your life that God is inviting you to. If this is true for you, express in your own words the reality that you long for, and use it as a springboard for prayer.

For the group

You may want to focus your discussion for lesson 2 especially on some of the following issues, themes, and concepts (which are recognized as major overall themes in 1 and 2 Chronicles). Which of these are dealt with in some way in chapters 8–12, and how are they further developed there?

- The meaning and significance of God's covenant relationship with His people
- God's nature, especially as revealed by how He acts in the details of His people's history
- The importance and meaning of worship
- For God's people, the continuity of the present with the past
- The importance of obedience to God's Word and His laws, and our personal responsibility in that regard
- How sin brings disaster and judgment from God

- God's continued blessings and grace for His people
- The future hope of God's people
- The unity of God's people
- God's sovereignty over His people's lives and history

The following numbered questions in lesson 2 may stimulate your best and most helpful discussion: 1, 5, 6, 7, 8, 10, 13, 14, 15, and 16.

Look also at the questions in the margins under the heading "For Thought and Discussion."

1. *New Geneva Study Bible* (Nashville: Thomas Nelson, 1995), introduction to 1 Chronicles, "Characteristics and Themes."
2. Andrew E. Hill, *1 & 2 Chronicles*, The NIV Application Commentary series, ed. Terry Much (Grand Rapids, MI: Zondervan, 2003), 49.
3. Hill, 200.
4. Hill, 201–202.
5. Hill, 202.

1 CHRONICLES 13-20

The Reign of David

1. In one sitting if possible, read attentively all of 1 Chronicles 13–20, taking notes and underlining or highlighting as you go. What impresses you overall as the key features and themes of this part of the book?

_____

_____

_____

_____

Chapters 13–16 tell how King David installed the ark of the covenant in Jerusalem and longed to build a "house" worthy of the Lord's great Name. Then chapter 17 tells how the Lord intended to build David's "house" into a royal line worthy of the Lord's great Name.

2. In chapter 13, what are the most important factors and perspectives regarding the story of the ark?

Let us bring the ark of our God back to us, for we did not inquire of it during the reign of Saul (13:3). The purpose of moving the ark is for the whole nation to draw closer to God and depend on Him.

Enthroned between the cherubim (13:6). The ark was a wooden chest. Its lid was covered in gold leaf, and golden statues of cherubim (angelic beings) stood on each end of the lid. The ark was the throne for God's usually invisible but awe-inspiring presence. This was where God chose to meet with and guide His people (see Exodus 25:22). In ancient Middle Eastern art, cherubim were depicted as lions or bulls with wings and human faces.

3. What do you see about David's heart and character in chapter 13?

_____

_____

_____

_____

Then David was angry. . . . David was afraid of God (13:11-12). David thinks the Lord capriciously attacked an innocent man. But in fact, the Lord's innate holiness makes Him dangerous for any mere human to approach without taking extreme care. Only the Levites are allowed to carry the holy things of the tabernacle, and even they have to use polls fitted in rings to carry the ark so as to avoid touching it, on pain of death (see Numbers 4:15). David doesn't know this, but he realizes he is dealing with someone far beyond his understanding and control.

For Further Study:
Compare 1 Chronicles 14:1-17 to the parallel account in 2 Samuel 5:11-25.

4. In chapter 14, what are the most important factors and perspectives regarding David's success as king?

_____

_____

_____

_____

The sound of marching in the tops of the poplar trees (14:15). The wind rustling the leaves is probably God's Spirit. ("Wind" and "spirit" are the same word in Hebrew.) The noise like soldiers marching will bewilder the enemy.[1]

5. In chapters 15 and 16, what are the most important factors and perspectives regarding the establishment of formal worship of the Lord in Jerusalem?

_____

_____

_____

_____

6. What is the significance of the confession and acknowledgment made by David in 15:13?

_____

_____

_____

_____

For Thought and Discussion: From what you're seeing so far in 1 Chronicles, how would you describe David's relationship with God?

For Further Study: Compare 1 Chronicles 15:25–16:6 to the parallel account in 2 Samuel 6:12-19.

We did not inquire of him about how to do it in the prescribed way (15:13). The Law of Moses explains the prescribed way, but no one consulted it.

Michal daughter of Saul (15:29). Her indifference toward the things of God gives one final reason why God rejected the house of Saul.[2]

The tent that David had pitched (16:1). Not the tabernacle of Moses, which is still apparently at Gibeon (see 16:39; 21:29).[3] Having the ark in Jerusalem solidifies God's rule over the kingdom and Israel's commitment to the covenant.

---

7. What specifically does David exhort the people to do in 16:8-13, and what is the significance of this?

_____

_____

_____

_____

_____

_____

> David's thanksgiving psalm in 16:8-36 expresses the core themes of the history the Chronicler is telling.[4]

8. What does David emphasize about God's character in 16:14-22?

_____

_____

_____

_____

_____

He remembers his covenant forever . . . the covenant he made with Abraham (16:15-16). The covenants with Abraham, Moses, and David are central to the Chronicler's version of his people's history. See also 2 Chronicles 6:14; 7:18; 21:7; 34:30-32.

9. In 16:23-30, notice *who* David addresses, the specific commands he gives them, and the reasons for the commands. What timeless significance do you see here?

_____

_____

_____

_____

10. Chapter 17 has been called the key to the book of 1 Chronicles. Why might this be so?

_____

_____

_____

_____

11. What are the most important truths God communicates to David in 17:3-15?

_____

_____

_____

_____

I will establish his kingdom. He is the one who will build a house for me, and I will establish his throne forever (17:11-12). For the Chronicler, the two institutions his nation needs to be fully restored are the temple in Jerusalem and a king from the line of David. Judah has a temple; she needs a Davidic king.

For Thought and Discussion: What are the most important worship principles you see illustrated in chapters 15 and 16?

For Further Study: How does David's thanksgiving psalm in 1 Chronicles 16:8-36 compare with Psalms 96; 105:1-15; 106?

Optional Application: What parts of David's thanksgiving psalm in 1 Chronicles 16:8-36 are most meaningful to you now in your own worship of the Lord?

Optional Application: Note especially David's words of instruction to the people in 1 Chronicles 16:11-12. What personal relevance does this have for you in your current circumstances?

For Further Study:
Compare 1 Chronicles
17 to the parallel
account in 2 Samuel 7.

**Optional
Application:** In
what ways is David's
prayer in 1 Chronicles
17:16-27 a model for
your own prayers?
What spiritual signifi-
cance does this have
for you in the present
circumstances of your
life?

For Further Study:
As you reflect on the
eternal kingdom that
God promised to
David's descendants
in 1 Chronicles 17,
consider how these
kingdom promises
are fulfilled in Christ.
See Luke 1:32; Acts
2:33-35; Romans
1:3; 5:19; 8:37-39;
1 Corinthians 15:24-26;
Ephesians 1:20-23;
4:7-13; Philippians
2:8-9; Hebrews 5:7-10;
Revelation 3:21; 22:16.
How do these pas-
sages deepen your
understanding of
God's promises to
David in 1 Chronicles
17?

12. What does David's prayer in 17:16-27 reveal
    most about his love for God and his under-
    standing of God?

    _____

    _____

    _____

    _____

King David went in and sat before the LORD
(17:16). David went into the tent-sanctuary and
sat there to pray. There must have been a place
there where a non-priest was allowed to enter
for prayer. Given what David saw when Uzzah
mishandled the ark, he is brave to approach
God so closely.

---

13. In chapter 17, how would you summarize what
    David learns most about God?

    _____

    _____

    _____

    _____

The account of David's military campaigns
in chapters 18–20 shows why God didn't
permit David to build the temple. David has
"shed much blood" (22:8; 28:3). God would
choose a dwelling place when Israel had
"rest" from her enemies (Deuteronomy
12:10; 25:19), and in David's time she was
still at war.[5]

14. In chapters 18–20, what are the most important factors and perspectives regarding David's military campaigns and victories?

_____

_____

_____

_____

For Further Study: Compare 1 Chronicles 18 to the parallel account in 2 Samuel 8–9.

For Further Study: Compare 1 Chronicles 19 to the parallel account in 2 Samuel 10.

For Further Study: Compare 1 Chronicles 20:1-3 to the parallel account in 2 Samuel 11:1; 12:26-31.

For Further Study: Compare 1 Chronicles 20:4-8 to the parallel account in 2 Samuel 21:15-22.

The LORD gave David victory wherever he went (18:6,13). The implication is that the Lord will also give victory to the Chronicler's generation if they are similarly dedicated to restoring the nation physically and spiritually.[6]

Doing what was just and right for all his people (18:14). The standard for evaluating a king.

The LORD will do what is good in his sight (19:13). Or "may the Lord do what seems good to him" (ESV). Joab is offering a prayer that entrusts the battle to the Lord's goodness.[7]

In the spring, at the time when kings go off to war. . . . But David remained in Jerusalem (20:1). See 2 Samuel 11–12. The Chronicler leaves out the story of David's sin with Bathsheba, probably because he wants to emphasize David's qualities of ideal kingship. He also wants to motivate his readers to perseverance by emphasizing how David's army succeeds despite incredible obstacles. But his readers know the dark story of David's sin and will be reminded by the mention of David's remaining in the city.

Optional Application: On the basis of God's truth revealed to you in this lesson, perhaps the Holy Spirit has helped you sense a new and higher reality in your life that God is inviting you to. If this is true for you, express in your own words the reality that you long for, and use it as a springboard for prayer.

15. How would you evaluate David's leadership as evidenced in chapters 18–20?

_____

_____

_____

16. What timeless spiritual principles do you see emphasized in the details of Israel's history as recorded in 1 Chronicles 13–20?

_____

_____

_____

_____

17. How would you summarize the most important perspectives these chapters give us about the man David?

_____

_____

_____

18. In 1 Chronicles 13–20, what would you select as the key verse or passage — one that best captures or reflects the dynamics of what these chapters are all about?

_____

_____

_____

19. List any lingering questions you have about 1 Chronicles 13–20.

_____

_____

_____

_____

For the group

You may want to focus your discussion for lesson 3 especially on some of the following issues, themes, and concepts (which are recognized as major overall themes in 1 and 2 Chronicles). Which of these are dealt with in some way in chapters 13–20, and how are they further developed there?

- The meaning and significance of God's covenant relationship with His people
- God's nature, especially as revealed by how He acts in the details of His people's history
- The importance and meaning of worship
- For God's people, the continuity of the present with the past
- The importance of obedience to God's Word and His laws, and our personal responsibility in that regard
- How sin brings disaster and judgment from God
- God's continued blessings and grace for His people
- The future hope of God's people
- The unity of God's people
- God's sovereignty over His people's lives and history

The following numbered questions in lesson 3 may stimulate your best and most helpful discussion: 1, 3, 4, 7, 9, 10, 11, 12, 14, 15, 16, 17, 18, and 19.

Remember to look also at the "For Thought and Discussion" questions in the margins.

1. Andrew E. Hill, *1 & 2 Chronicles*, The NIV Application Commentary series, ed. Terry Much (Grand Rapids, MI: Zondervan, 2003), 233.
2. Hill, 237.
3. Hill, 237.
4. Hill, 237.
5. Hill, 257.
6. Hill, 260.
7. Hill, 264.

Lesson Four

1 CHRONICLES 21–27

David's Later Days

1. Proverbs 2:1-5 tells about the sincere person who truly longs for wisdom and understanding and who searches the Scriptures for it as if there were treasure buried there. Such a person, this passage says, will come to understand the fear of the Lord and discover the knowledge of God. As you continue exploring 1 Chronicles, what "hidden treasure" would you like God to help you find here to show you what He and His wisdom are really like? If you have this desire, how would you express it in your own words of prayer to God?

For Thought and Discussion: What are you learning so far from your study of 1 Chronicles about God's character and personality?

_____

_____

_____

_____

_____

2. In one sitting if possible, read attentively all of 1 Chronicles 21–27, taking notes and underlining or highlighting as you go. What impresses you overall as the key features and themes of this part of the book?

For Further Study:
Compare 1 Chronicles
21:1–22:5 to the
parallel account in
2 Samuel 24.

3. Summarize what happens in the life of David
and the nation of Israel in chapter 21 and
explain its significance. What is the major point
God is making by including this chapter in the
Bible?

_____

_____

_____

_____

_____

Satan . . . incited David (21:1). The writer of
2 Samuel says the Lord incited David (see
2 Samuel 24:1). Both are true. The Lord used
Satan to test David, and David fell for the bait.
David is responsible for his wrong choice. Satan
is responsible for doing evil. The Lord is sovereign over both and has redemptive goals in
allowing humans to be tested.

4. What does chapter 21 reveal about the power of
repentance?

_____

_____

_____

_____

_____

_____

I have sinned greatly by doing this (21:8). It's not clear why it was sinful to take a census. Probably David's motive was flawed. The census of soldiers trumpeted David's military power rather than exalting God as Israel's only essential warrior.[1] God allowed war because Israel had enemies, but He rejected the glorification of violence. Israel was often victorious when badly outnumbered so that it was clear that God was the real fighter.

While Araunah was threshing wheat, he turned and saw the angel (21:20). "The destroying angel is already at the threshing floor, presumably ready to kill Araunah and his sons."[2] Time is of the essence.

5. How would you summarize what David learns most about God in chapter 21?

_____

_____

_____

_____

6. In chapter 22, what are the most important factors and perspectives regarding the temple and the worship of the Lord?

_____

_____

_____

_____

The house to be built for the LORD should be of great magnificence and fame and splendor in the sight of all the nations (22:5). The temple's beauty is not just for the pleasure of the Israelites. God chose Israel to be a blessing for the nations (see Genesis 12:3). The temple's beauty will proclaim that God is keeping His covenant promises.

For Further Study:
As you reflect on David's words to Solomon in 1 Chronicles 22:11-13, how does this transfer of royal authority compare with and reflect the commissioning of Joshua as the successor to Moses in Deuteronomy 31 and Joshua 1?

David's words to Solomon in 22:6-16 include both encouragement to complete the task and a prayer for God to help Solomon be a good king. God has called Solomon to do this great task, and God will give him the ability to do it. In the same way, God has called the people of the Chronicler's generation, and God will give them the ability to fulfill their calling.

A house for the Name of the LORD (22:7). "God's 'Name' stood for the glory-cloud of his presence in the tabernacle or the temple (Deuteronomy 12:11; 2 Chronicles 6:20)."[3] See also 1 Chronicles 29:16; 2 Chronicles 12:13.

---

7. Look closely at the reason God gives in 22:8 for not allowing David to build the temple. How would you explain this in your own words?

_____

_____

_____

_____

8. What promises for David and for Israel does God give in 22:9-10, and what is their significance?

_____

_____

_____

_____

_____

_____

Discretion and understanding (22:12). "Intelligence and insight." But true wisdom is linked to keeping the Lord's law.[4]

A hundred thousand talents of gold, a million talents of silver, quantities of bronze and iron too great to be weighed, and wood and stone (22:14). "Over forty thousand tons" of gold and silver. It would have had far greater purchasing power at that time than it would today.[5] This vast wealth can have come only from God's generous gift, so David means to spend it on God's house rather than on palaces for himself. David understands that God is of incalculable worth.

To help his son Solomon (22:17). This massive project will require the whole kingdom's support. There is a message here for the Chronicler's generation—all of them are needed to rebuild the nation.

Heart (22:19). This word occurs about three dozen times in 1 and 2 Chronicles. It's less the place of emotions than it is the place of desire and will and conscience. The people need to seek the Lord with their deepest desires, their focused will, and their conscience shaped by faith rather than selfishness.

Seeking the Lord your God (22:19). To "seek" God is to obey Him. It's not about guidance for one's personal life.[6]

9. In chapter 23, what are the most important aspects of the ministry of the Levites?

_____

_____

_____

_____

_____

_____

Optional Application: Notice especially the command David gives to the nation's leaders at the beginning of 1 Chronicles 22:19. In what ways is this also the Lord's personal word to you at this time? What are the most important ways for you to heed this command?

For Further Study:
For helpful background on the historical statement in 1 Chronicles 24:2, what do you discover in Leviticus 10:1-3?

Old and full of years (23:1). David is honored like Abraham (see Genesis 25:8), Isaac (see Genesis 35:29), and Moses (see Deuteronomy 34:7).[7]

Set apart (23:13). To make something holy is literally to set it apart. God's holiness is His "set-apartness." He is radically Other than the merely mortal. Aaron and his sons were transferred to that category of set-apartness so that they could minister with holy things to a holy God.

Man of God (23:14). One sent as God's prophet or agent. Moses' family did not inherit any special standing because of their illustrious ancestor.[8]

10. In chapter 24, what are the most important aspects of the ministry of the priests?

_____

_____

_____

_____

Nadab and Abihu died . . . so Eleazar and Ithamar served as the priests (24:2). The Chronicler's readers know that Nadab and Abihu died because of their sin. Eleazar and Ithamar lived because of their faithfulness and God's grace in providing a priestly lineage through the centuries to the Chronicler's own time.

11. In chapter 25, what are the most important factors and perspectives regarding the training and ministry of the temple musicians?

_____

_____

_____

12. What further factors and perspectives do you see emphasized in chapter 26 regarding the temple and the worship of the Lord?

_____

_____

_____

_____

Capable men with the strength to do the work
(26:8). The doors or gates to the temple area were huge and heavy, so strong men were needed to open and close them.[9]

13. In chapter 27, what are the most important factors and perspectives regarding leadership among God's people?

_____

_____

_____

_____

14. Look carefully at 27:23-24. How might this passage shed light on Joab's reaction to David's census in 1 Chronicles 21:1-3 and 2 Samuel 24:1-3?

_____

_____

_____

_____

The army divisions (27:1). Aggressive nations like Babylon and Persia kept large standing armies of professional soldiers. Israel's army was made

Optional Application: On the basis of God's truth revealed to you in this lesson, perhaps the Holy Spirit has helped you sense a new and higher reality in your life that God is inviting you to. If this is true for you, express in your own words the reality that you long for, and use it as a springboard for prayer.

up of citizens who served one month per year. It was more like our National Guard than our Army.[10] An army like this could be used only for defense, and even then it would have to rely on the Lord when aggressive nations threatened it.

The Lord had promised to make Israel as numerous as the stars in the sky (27:23). God's promise to Abraham (see Genesis 15:5). David needs to trust God to fulfill this promise and not count the fighting men in some faithless effort at control. It was crucial for the people and their leaders to know that "no king is saved by the size of his army" (Psalm 33:16). The people of the Chronicler's generation, too, needed to trust God and not worry about their small numbers.

---

15. What timeless spiritual principles do you see emphasized in the details of Israel's history as recorded in 1 Chronicles 21–27?

_____

_____

_____

_____

16. How would you summarize the most important teachings and perspectives that these chapters give us about the temple of God?

_____

_____

_____

_____

17. In 1 Chronicles 21–27, what would you select as the key verse or passage—one that best captures or reflects the dynamics of what these chapters are all about?

_____

_____

_____

_____

18. List any lingering questions you have about
    1 Chronicles 21–27.

_____

_____

_____

_____

For the group

You may want to focus your discussion for lesson 4
especially on some of the following issues, themes,
and concepts (which are recognized as major overall themes in 1 and 2 Chronicles). Which of these
are dealt with in some way in chapters 21–27, and
how are they further developed there?

- The meaning and significance of God's cov-
  enant relationship with His people
- God's nature, especially as revealed by how He
  acts in the details of His people's history
- The importance and meaning of worship
- For God's people, the continuity of the present
  with the past
- The importance of obedience to God's Word and
  His laws, and our personal responsibility in that
  regard
- How sin brings disaster and judgment from God
- God's continued blessings and grace for His
  people
- The future hope of God's people
- The unity of God's people
- God's sovereignty over His people's lives and
  history

   The following numbered questions in lesson 4
may stimulate your best and most helpful discussion: 2, 4, 5, 8, 13, 15, 16, 17, and 18.
   Remember to look also at the "For Thought and
Discussion" question in the margin.

1. Andrew E. Hill, *1 & 2 Chronicles*, The NIV Application Commentary series, ed. Terry Much (Grand Rapids, MI: Zondervan, 2003), 294.
2. Hill, 294.
3. J. Barton Payne, *1, 2 Chronicles*, vol. 4, The Expositor's Bible Commentary, ed. Frank E. Gaebelein (Grand Rapids, MI: Zondervan, 1988), 411.
4. Hill, 299.
5. Payne, 412.
6. Hill, 300.
7. Hill, 302.
8. Hill, 303.
9. Hill, 314.
10. Hill, 319.

Lesson Five

1 CHRONICLES 28–29; 2 CHRONICLES 1–5

The Rise of Solomon

1. In one sitting if possible, read attentively all of
   1 Chronicles 28–29 and 2 Chronicles 1–5, taking notes and underlining or highlighting as
   you go. What impresses you overall as the key
   features and themes of these chapters?

   _____

   _____

   _____

   _____

   _____

2. What are the specific charges that David gives
   to the people and his son Solomon in chapters
   28 and 29, and what is their significance?

   _____

   _____

   _____

   _____

   _____

   _____

   _____

Optional Application: What particular encouragement and exhortation for your personal walk with God do you see in the words of 1 Chronicles 28:9? In practical terms, what do you think serving God wholeheartedly means most for you at this time in your life?

Optional Application: Reflect on David's words to Solomon in 1 Chronicles 28:10. What unfinished work do you believe God has chosen *you* for?

For Further Study: As you examine David's God-given instructions for the temple in 1 Chronicles 28:11-19, how do these compare with the Lord's instructions for building the tabernacle in Exodus 25–30? What are the biggest similarities you see?

For the footstool of our God (28:2). A king's footstool represents his authority and his kingdom's "rest" from war and dissent. "Israel's 'rest' . . . is entwined with God's restful presence among his people."[1]

3. Summarize the "building of a house" theme as you've seen it developing in these passages of 1 Chronicles: 17:4,10,12,25; 22:5,11; 28:2-3.

_____

_____

_____

_____

Serve him with wholehearted devotion (28:9). Solomon will build the temple with wholehearted devotion, but in other ways his devotion to God is not wholehearted. He will be enticed by the foreign religions of the excessive number of wives he collects in his harem (see 1 Kings 11:4,6). His divided heart will lead to the division of his kingdom when his son inherits the throne.

Plans . . . plan (28:11,12,18,19). The pattern God gave for the tabernacle's design (see Exodus 25:9,40). David is like Moses in being God's agent to convey the design and found the house of worship.[2]

4. What action on the part of God's Spirit do you see in 28:12, and what does this passage tell us about how the Holy Spirit works?

_____

_____

_____

_____

_____

_____

He enabled me to understand all the details of the plan (28:19). The plan — the whole project — is God's.

Priests and Levites . . . and every willing person . . . officials and all the people (28:21). This will be a labor of love for God by the religious leaders, the political leaders, the craftsmen and women, and all the people.[3]

5. What significance do you see in the responses of the people to David in chapter 29?

_____

_____

_____

_____

6. How does David's speech to "the whole assembly" of Israel in 29:1-5 compare with his earlier speeches to this group in 22:2-19 and 28:1-21? What different emphasis do you see in each address?

_____

_____

_____

_____

_____

_____

_____

They had given freely and wholeheartedly to the LORD (29:9). Again we have the reference to the

For Further Study:
Notice again in
1 Chronicles 29:6-9
how the people gave
freely and gener-
ously for the building
of the temple. Then
compare this to how
their ancestors gave
for the building of the
tabernacle in Exodus
35:20-29. What are
the biggest similari-
ties you see in these
two accounts, and
what principles can
you draw from them
about our giving
to the Lord's work
today?

heart. Building the temple will be as much an
act of worship as singing and praying and offering sacrifice within it.

7. What timeless principles for worship and service to the Lord do you see in 29:1-22?

8. What does David's prayer in 29:10-19 reveal
most about his understanding of God?

I know, my God, that you test the heart (29:17).
God tests not the emotions but the motives,
the will, and the conscience of each person.
These tests are necessary for spiritual health.

9. In 29:22-30, what do these final verses in
1 Chronicles emphasize about David and
Solomon?

10. As we come to the close of the Chronicler's
account of the life of David, what are the most
important developments in his life that are set
forth in this book?

_____

_____

_____

_____

The Chronicler seems to model his account of the transition from David to Solomon on the biblical account of the transition from Moses to Joshua.

"a. Both David and Moses fail to attain their goals — one to build the temple and the other to enter the promised land. In both cases the divine prohibition is related to the appointment of a successor (1 Chronicles 22:5-13; 28:2-8; Deuteronomy 1:37-38; 31:2-8).

"b. Both Solomon and Joshua bring the people of God into rest (1 Chronicles 22:8-9; Joshua 11:23; 21:44).

"c. There are a number of verbal parallels in the appointments of Solomon and Joshua (compare 1 Chronicles 22:11-13,16; 28:7-10,20; 2 Chronicles 1:1 with Deuteronomy 31:5-8,23; Joshua 1:5,7-9).

"d. There are both private and public announcements of the appointment of the successors: private (1 Chronicles 22:6; Deuteronomy 31:23); public (1 Chronicles 28:8; Deuteronomy 31:7 — both 'in the presence/sight of all Israel').

"e. Both enjoy the immediate and whole-hearted support of the people (1 Chronicles 29:23-24; Deuteronomy 34:9; Joshua 1:16-18).

"f. It is twice reported that God 'exalted' or 'made great' Solomon and Joshua (1 Chronicles 29:25; 2 Chronicles 1:1; Joshua 3:7; 4:14)."[4]

11. What are the most important points and perspectives communicated in the exchange between the Lord and Solomon in 2 Chronicles 1?

_____

_____

Optional Application: Reflect deeply on David's prayer in 1 Chronicles 29:10-19 as it relates to your own attitude in worship of the Lord. In particular, how does your own heart measure up to the standards David refers to in verses 17-19?

For Further Study: Reflect further on God's testing of the heart that David mentions in 1 Chronicles 29:17. How do you see this principle affirmed in James 1:3-8, 2 Corinthians 13:5, and Galatians 6:4?

Optional Application: Think again about David's acknowledgment in 1 Chronicles 29:17 of how the Lord tests our hearts. How is the Lord testing your own heart at this time?

For Further Study: Compare 1 Chronicles 29:20-25 to the parallel account in 1 Kings 1:28-40.

For Further Study: Compare 1 Chronicles 29:26-30 to the parallel account in 1 Kings 2:10-11.

For Thought and Discussion: What do the early chapters of 2 Chronicles reveal most about Solomon's character?

For Further Study: Compare 2 Chronicles 1:1-12 to the parallel account in 1 Kings 3:4-14.

For Further Study: Compare 2 Chronicles 1:14-17 to the parallel account in 1 Kings 4:20-34.

For Thought and Discussion: If God asked you the same question He asked Solomon in 2 Chronicles 1:7, how would you answer?

_____
_____

Exceedingly great (1:1). David wanted to build a house for God, and God instead built David's royal house. Likewise, Solomon set out to build a temple to make God's Name great among the nations, and God made Solomon's name great.[5]

12. From what you see in this chapter and elsewhere, how well did God do in fulfilling His promises to Solomon in 1:12?

_____
_____
_____
_____

13. What are the most important actions Solomon takes in chapter 1?

_____
_____
_____
_____

Chariots and horses . . . silver and gold . . . horses (1:14-16). This account of Solomon's wealth is repeated in 9:25-28 at the end of the account of Solomon. Solomon's story is thus framed with a summary of his wealth to show that God was faithful to His promise in 1:12.[6] Horses and chariots were the military hardware of their day. Solomon was a man of peace, but he amassed the equivalent of tanks and missiles as a display of his splendor. This was not a good example for his successors.

14. In chapter 2, what are the most important factors and perspectives regarding the preparations for building the temple?

_____

_____

_____

_____

Temple (2:1). This word occurs more often in 2 Chronicles than in any other book of the Bible. Notice especially the perspectives on the temple as given in 2:5-6; 5:13-14; 6:18-21; 7:1-3,12,16,20-22; 29:3-8; 33:7-9.

15. Notice the observation King Hiram—a foreigner—makes about God's people in 2:11. How do you think he came to this conclusion?

_____

_____

_____

16. In chapter 3, what are the most important factors and perspectives regarding the actual construction of the temple?

_____

_____

_____

_____

Overlaid . . . with gold . . . carved cherubim (3:7). This is the throne room and audience halls of the King of glory, with the gold of heaven on the walls and ceiling, and angelic beings carved along the walls. The ark of the

For Further Study: Compare 2 Chronicles 2 to the parallel account in 1 Kings 5.

For Further Study: Second Chronicles 3:1 describes the place in Jerusalem where Solomon built the temple. What background information can you discover about this place from Genesis 22:1-18 and 2 Samuel 24:18-25 (paralleled in 1 Chronicles 21:18–22:1)?

For Thought and Discussion: It's often said that a person's home is a reflection of his personality. From what you see in 2 Chronicles 3 and 4, how would the temple be a reflection of God's personality?

For Further Study: Compare 2 Chronicles 3–4 to the parallel account in 1 Kings 6–7.

For Further Study: Compare 2 Chronicles 5 to the parallel account in 1 Kings 8:1-11.

covenant with its cherubim would never be seen except by the high priest, in the Most Holy Place, but the other priests would see the golden outer rooms.

The Most Holy Place (3:10). Shaped in a perfect cube to represent God's perfection. No lamp burned in this windowless space, and a heavy curtain over the door shut out all light. The ark, God's throne, was there in the darkness. Did God's glory burn there visibly between the cherubim when the high priest brought the blood of the sacrifice on the Day of Atonement? Or did the priest do his work in the dark, seen only by the all-seeing God?

17. In chapter 4, what are the most important factors and perspectives regarding the furnishing of the temple?

_____

_____

_____

_____

18. In chapter 5, what are the most important factors and perspectives regarding the bringing of the ark into the temple?

_____

_____

_____

_____

Nothing in the ark except the two tablets that Moses had placed in it at Horeb (5:10). A jar of manna and Aaron's staff (which had budded and borne almonds during Israel's time in the wilderness) were set before the ark (see Exodus 16:32-34; Numbers 17:10-11). At some point those items were placed inside the ark (see Hebrews 9:4).

He is good; his love endures forever (5:13). A sung refrain used in Psalm 136 and in various celebrations in Chronicles (see 1 Chronicles 16:34,41; 2 Chronicles 7:3,6; 20:21). The word for "love" here means loyalty to the covenant relationship.

19. In 1 Chronicles 28–29 and 2 Chronicles 1–5, what would you select as the key verse or passage—one that best captures or reflects the dynamics of what these chapters are all about?

_____

_____

_____

_____

20. What timeless spiritual principles do you see emphasized in the details of Israel's history as recorded in these chapters?

_____

_____

_____

_____

21. List any lingering questions you have about this lesson's Scripture text.

_____

_____

_____

_____

Optional Application: On the basis of God's truth revealed to you in this lesson, perhaps the Holy Spirit has helped you sense a new and higher reality in your life that God is inviting you to. If this is true for you, express in your own words the reality that you long for, and use it as a springboard for prayer.

For the group

You may want to focus your discussion for lesson 5 especially on some of the following issues, themes, and concepts (which are recognized as major overall themes in 1 and 2 Chronicles). Which of these are dealt with in some way in this lesson's Scripture text (1 Chronicles 28–29 and 2 Chronicles 1–5), and how are they further developed there?

* The meaning and significance of God's covenant relationship with His people
* God's nature, especially as revealed by how He acts in the details of His people's history
* The importance and meaning of worship
* For God's people, the continuity of the present with the past
* The importance of obedience to God's Word and His laws, and our personal responsibility in that regard
* How sin brings disaster and judgment from God
* God's continued blessings and grace for His people
* The future hope of God's people
* The unity of God's people
* God's sovereignty over His people's lives and history

The following numbered questions in lesson 5 may stimulate your best and most helpful discussion: 1, 2, 7, 8, 9, 10, 11, 12, 19, 20, and 21.

Remember to look also at the "For Thought and Discussion" questions in the margins.

1. Andrew E. Hill, *1 & 2 Chronicles*, The NIV Application Commentary series, ed. Terry Much (Grand Rapids, MI: Zondervan, 2003), 323.
2. Hill, 325.
3. Hill, 327.
4. *NIV Study Bible* (Grand Rapids, MI: Zondervan, 1985), introduction to 1 Chronicles: "Portrait of David and Solomon."
5. Hill, 377.
6. Hill, 381–382.

2 CHRONICLES 6–9

The Reign of Solomon

These chapters "devoted to the temple are like waves coming on the shore, with each wave higher than the preceding one."[1]

---

1. In one sitting if possible, read attentively all of 2 Chronicles 6–9, taking notes and underlining or highlighting as you go. What impresses you overall as the key features and themes of this part of the book?

   _____

   _____

   _____

   _____

In 2 Chronicles 6, we witness the dedication of the temple. "There is no grander chapter in the Bible than this one. Solomon the king, as representative of the nation, conducts himself with a stateliness and speaks with a formality that the occasion demands."[2]

Optional Application: How can Solomon's words of blessing and prayer in chapter 6 best serve as a model for your own worship and prayer?

For Further Study: Compare 2 Chronicles 6 to the parallel account in 1 Kings 8:12-61.

Optional Application: What encouragement and exhortation for your personal walk with God do you see in the words of 2 Chronicles 6:14?

2. What are the most important points Solomon makes in his words of blessing in 6:1-11?

_____

_____

_____

_____

Since the day I brought my people out of Egypt (6:5). Solomon links God's covenant with David (by which God promised that David's royal dynasty would rule forever) with His covenant through Moses (by which God rescued the nation from Egypt and gave her laws). The two covenants are linked and equally reliable.[3]

3. In Solomon's prayer of dedication for the temple in 6:12-42, what do you see as his most significant requests?

_____

_____

_____

_____

Hear the supplications . . . and when you hear, forgive (6:21). The temple is not simply a place of sacrifice to atone for sin. The sacrifices are alluded to, but Solomon emphasizes that the temple is a place of prayer. Prayer for the forgiveness of sin is uppermost in his mind (see 6:25,27,30,39). Sin will be the root of troubles Israel may face. If sin is confessed, atoned for, and forgiven, then God's ears will be open to hear other prayers.

4. What does 2 Chronicles 6 reveal most about Solomon's understanding of God's personality and character?

_____

_____

_____

_____

5. Reflect on 7:1-10. What do these verses reveal most about the Lord and about His people at this moment in history?

_____

_____

_____

For Further Study:
Look again at what God did in 2 Chronicles 7:1-3, and compare it with what He did in Exodus 40:34-35 and Leviticus 9:23-24. What are the biggest similarities in these incidents, and what do you think God wants us to understand most about them?

The glory of the LORD filled the temple (7:1). The presence of God, manifested in a cloud by day and fire by night during Israel's time in the wilderness (see Exodus 13:21). Just before the Babylonians later destroyed Solomon's temple and all of Jerusalem with it, Ezekiel had a vision of the glory abandoning the defiled temple (see Ezekiel 10:3-5,18-19).

The good things the LORD had done for David and Solomon and for his people Israel (7:10). For the Chronicler, David and Solomon weren't the source of Israel's peace and prosperity. They were agents through whom God gave those blessings.[4]

6. What particular significance do you see in the statement made in 7:11?

_____

_____

_____

_____

_____

**Optional
Application:** The
famous words in
2 Chronicles 7:14 have
been called the great-
est prescription for
revival in any land. At
this time, how is God
speaking through
these words to you
and your church?

The LORD appeared to him at night (7:12). The
Lord appeared to Solomon at night at Gibeon
too (see 1:7-12). Now thirteen years have
passed, and Solomon has built a palace for the
Lord and a palace for himself. The Lord tells
him how to live, and the Chronicler omits mention of the ways Solomon fell short.

*If my people . . . will humble themselves and
pray and seek my face and turn from their
wicked ways* (7:14). A process of repentance
with four steps: humbling ("to subdue one's
pride and submit . . . to God and his will,"),
praying ("a shameless acknowledgment of
personal sin and a plea for God's mercy" as
in Psalm 51:1-2), seeking (setting all of one's
hopes on God and choosing Him above all else),
and turning (changing the direction of one's
actions away from sin and toward God's way).[5]

Second Chronicles 7:14 summarizes the
theme of the rest of 2 Chronicles. The
Chronicler will note the promising
moments when the later kings and
people of Judah humble themselves (see
Rehoboam in 12:6-7), pray repentantly
(see Hezekiah in 32:20), seek God as their
only hope (see Jehoshaphat and the
people of Judah in 20:3-4), and turn away
from sin to obey God's laws (see Asa
and the people in 15:4).[6] The Chronicler
will also note kings who fail to do those
things. Those who repent are forgiven
and prosper, while those who don't
repent are responsible for God's tragic
final decision to send the Babylonians.

7. From what you see in 7:12-22, what does the
Lord most want Solomon to remember and
understand at this time?

_____

_____

_____

_____

_____

8. What do God's words to Solomon in chapter 7 reveal about the power of repentance?

_____

_____

_____

9. In chapter 8, what are the most important factors and perspectives regarding Solomon's success as king?

_____

_____

_____

_____

My wife must not live in the palace ... because the places the ark of the Lord has entered are holy (8:11). For the first twenty years of his reign, Solomon was concerned about obeying the Lord and respecting the purity of places He had made holy. The Chronicler omits mention of the later years of Solomon's reign, when he accumulated seven hundred wives and three hundred concubines in his harem, from pagan nations, and built shrines for their gods (see 1 Kings 11:5-8). The Chronicler wants Solomon to represent the good kingship of the temple builder. However, "then, as now, ritual purity was not a one-time event ... but an ongoing process of applying the biblical teaching about God's holiness to daily living."[7]

For Further Study: Compare 2 Chronicles 7:4-22 to the parallel account in 1 Kings 8:62–9:9.

Optional Application: What personal encouragement and exhortation for your own walk with God do you see in the Lord's words to Solomon in 2 Chronicles 7:14?

For Further Study: As you reflect on the Chronicles narrative about the construction and dedication of the temple, look to these New Testament passages to see how the purposes of the temple are fulfilled in Jesus Christ: John 14:1-4; 1 Thessalonians 4:16-17; Hebrews 3:1; 4:14-16; 6:20; 7:26; 8:1; 9:11-28; 1 Peter 3:18; 1 John 2:2. What do you see as the most significant ways that Jesus fulfills God's purposes for the temple?

For Further Study: Compare 2 Chronicles 8 to the parallel account in 1 Kings 9:10-28.

Lesson Six

For Further Study:

For Further Study:
Compare 2 Chronicles
9 to the parallel
account in 1 Kings
10:1-29; 11:41-43.

10. How does chapter 9 emphasize God's blessing
on Solomon?

_____

_____

_____

_____

11. What observation does the queen of Sheba—a
foreigner—make about God and His people
in 9:8? How do you think she came to this
conclusion?

_____

_____

_____

_____

_____

Queen of Sheba (9:1). Jesus points to her as an
example of a non-Jew who journeyed a great
distance to hear Solomon's wisdom, while
the Jews of His own day dismissed the teaching of a King far greater than King Solomon
(Matthew 12:42). Solomon's grandeur and
wisdom are thus signs pointing toward his
greater descendant.

Lions (9:18-19). A symbol of kingship at that time,
and possibly the symbol of the house of David.
David was famous for having rescued sheep
from a lion (see 1 Samuel 17:34-37).[8]

Solomon was greater in riches (9:22). For the
Chronicler, Solomon's wealth was evidence of
God's faithfulness to His promises. But Jesus
minimized Solomon's splendor, saying that it
was nothing compared to the splendor of wild-
flowers (see Matthew 6:28-34). For Jesus, God's
faithfulness to Solomon should not move us
to focus on possessions. Jesus said to pursue
God's kingdom and His righteousness and

68

trust God to give us any necessary material things along the way.

He rested with his ancestors (9:31). This phrase sums up a picture of peace and prosperity, an ideal kingship. The Chronicler leaves out the negative details in 1 Kings 11.[9]

12. What timeless spiritual principles do you see emphasized in the details of Israel's history as recorded in 2 Chronicles 6–9?

_____

_____

_____

_____

13. In 2 Chronicles 6–9, what would you select as the key verse or passage—one that best captures or reflects the dynamics of what these chapters are all about?

_____

_____

_____

_____

14. List any lingering questions you have about 2 Chronicles 6–9.

_____

_____

_____

_____

For the group

You may want to focus your discussion for lesson 6 especially on some of the following issues, themes, and concepts (which are recognized as

For Thought and Discussion: If you could go back in time and God brought you into the events of these chapters to act as a royal adviser to King Solomon, what kind of counsel would you give him, and how would you express it?

For Further Study: In telling Solomon's story, the writer of Chronicles has omitted much of what is included in 1 Kings. Read these omissions in 1 Kings 1:1-27; 2:13-46; 11:1-40. The author of Chronicles and the author of 1 Kings appear to have different purposes in their portrayals of Solomon. How would you describe these different purposes?

Optional Application: On the basis of God's truth revealed to you in this lesson, perhaps the Holy Spirit has helped you sense a new and higher reality in your life that God is inviting you to. If this is true for you, express in your own words the reality that you long for, and use it as a springboard for prayer.

major overall themes in 1 and 2 Chronicles). Which of these are dealt with in some way in chapters 6–9, and how are they further developed there?

- The meaning and significance of God's covenant relationship with His people
- God's nature, especially as revealed by how He acts in the details of His people's history
- The importance and meaning of worship
- For God's people, the continuity of the present with the past
- The importance of obedience to God's Word and His laws, and our personal responsibility in that regard
- How sin brings disaster and judgment from God
- God's continued blessings and grace for His people
- The future hope of God's people
- The unity of God's people
- God's sovereignty over His people's lives and history

   The following numbered questions in lesson 6 may stimulate your best and most helpful discussion: 1, 2, 3, 4, 7, 8, 13, and 14.

   Once more, look also at the question in the margin under the heading "For Thought and Discussion."

1. Leland Ryken and Philip Graham Ryken, eds., *The Literary Study Bible* (Wheaton, IL: Crossway, 2007), at 1 Chronicles 7.
2. Ryken and Ryken, at 1 Chronicles 6.
3. Andrew E. Hill, *1 & 2 Chronicles*, The NIV Application Commentary series, ed. Terry Much (Grand Rapids, MI: Zondervan, 2003), 392.
4. Hill, 398.
5. Hill, 400.
6. Hill, 400.
7. Hill, 404.
8. Hill, 409.
9. Hill, 411.

2 CHRONICLES 10–16

The Kingdom Divided

The building of the temple is the high point of the Chronicler's story. After Solomon, the northern tribes rebelled against Solomon's son, and the nation split in two: Israel in the north and Judah in the south. The Chronicler focuses his attention on Judah, because that is where Jerusalem and the temple were located, and that is where the Jews returned after the exile. The books of 1 and 2 Kings also deal with the fate of the northern kingdom, but Chronicles omits most of that material.

The rest of 2 Chronicles (chapters 10–36) follows the kings of Judah down to the Babylonian exile. King David — and to a lesser degree King Solomon — is the standard by which the various kings are evaluated. The Chronicler tells how the king did good or evil, especially whether the king kept the commands of Moses' covenant and how the king treated temple worship. He connects that behavior with the judgment or blessing God sends on the nation. He emphasizes the judgment or blessing the kings experienced in their lifetime rather than constantly pointing toward the great judgment of the exile. In the case of bad kings, the Chronicler notes that God withheld His full wrath because of the covenant He had made with David (see 2 Chronicles 21:7).

1. In one sitting if possible, read attentively all of 2 Chronicles 10–16, taking notes and underlining or highlighting as you go. What impresses you overall as the key features and themes of this part of the book?

_____

_____

_____

_____

Israel's unity ("all Israel") is enormously important to the Chronicler, so the division of the nation is a huge tragedy for him. The most tragic moment is when Rehoboam rejects the advice of the elders on how to respond to the concerns of the northern tribes (see 10:6-11). Never again, up to the Chronicler's day, will all Israel be one nation as it should be.

2. What evidence do you see in chapter 10 for the causes of the sudden breakup of the kingdom after Solomon's death? Who was most to blame for this breakup?

For Thought and Discussion: If you were an adviser to King Rehoboam, what would you counsel him to do differently from what he did in chapter 10?

_____
_____
_____
_____

Your father put a heavy yoke on us (10:4). Much of Solomon's wealth came from tribute paid by other nations, but he did tax the people for the maintenance of his lavish palace, his enormous harem of a thousand women, his thousands of horses (see 1 Kings 4:22-28), and the bureaucracy of government (see 1 Kings 9:22-23). The northern tribes wanted Rehoboam to reduce the taxation. So Solomon, Rehoboam, and Jeroboam all bear responsibility for the nation's breakup.

Rejecting the advice of the elders, he followed the advice of the young men (10:13-14). Rehoboam is forty-one years old (see 12:13) — not a young man himself, but accustomed to being the spoiled crown prince with plenty of privileges and no practice in governing. He doesn't know how to reduce government spending effectively, and he doesn't want to look weak.[1]

All the Israelites went home. But as for the Israelites who were living in the towns of Judah (10:16-17). The Chronicler still calls both the northerners and the people of Judah "Israelites." For him, spiritually speaking, the chosen people are still one nation.[2]

Rebellion . . . to this day (10:19). The northerners rebelled against the house of David and against God, who gave the covenant with David. In the Chronicler's day, the northern kingdom had ceased to exist, and an ethnically mixed population with a mixed religion lived in that region. But for the Chronicler, the ten tribes weren't gone; they were just still in rebellion.

For Further Study: Compare 2 Chronicles 10–11 to the parallel account in 1 Kings 12.

For Thought and Discussion: As you explore the events of chapter 12, discuss how much you agree or disagree with this statement: In God's perspective, the responsibility for His people's obedience rested mainly on the shoulders of the king.

For Further Study: Compare 2 Chronicles 12:1-12 to the parallel account in 1 Kings 14:25-28.

3. Summarize the beginning of Rehoboam's reign as narrated in chapter 11. What were the most important achievements of his reign?

_____

_____

_____

_____

4. What is the particular theological significance and spiritual instruction of the information given in 11:16-17?

_____

_____

_____

_____

5. What aspects of King Rehoboam's reign are emphasized in chapter 12, and what is their significance?

_____

_____

_____

_____

_____

_____

[Rehoboam] and all Israel with him abandoned the law of the LORD (12:1). The Chronicler speaks of the people of Judah, from whichever tribe, as "all Israel" because for him, those who still obey the house of David are the true Israel.[3]

Because they had been unfaithful to the LORD, Shishak king of Egypt attacked Jerusalem (12:2). The Chronicler sees God as the "Lord of

74

history,"4 sending immediate judgment on the people for their sin.

For Further Study:
Compare 2 Chronicles 12:13-16 to the parallel account in 1 Kings 14:21-24,29-31.

6. What does chapter 12 reveal about the power of repentance?

_____

_____

_____

_____

Humbled himself (12:12). Recall 7:14. The heart flaw that motivated Rehoboam to make a bad decision that split the nation (see chapter 10) was pride. The heart flaw that motivated Rehoboam to forsake God's law (see 12:1) was pride. Here Rehoboam turns away from his pride and chooses God, and as 7:14 promised, God hears him. The Chronicler wants this to be a message for the leaders and people of his day.

---

7. What is the particular theological significance and spiritual instruction of the information given in 12:14?

_____

_____

_____

_____

8. As recorded in chapter 13, how would you summarize the military developments in the fighting between Israel and Judah? And what is the significance of verse 18 in regard to this conflict?

_____

_____

_____

For Further Study:
Compare 2 Chronicles 13 to the parallel account in 1 Kings 15:1-8.

Optional Application: In 2 Chronicles 13, look at the confident words Abijah spoke at the beginning of verse 10 and the beginning of verse 12. Could these words be spoken with the same confidence today by you and the people in your church? Why or why not?

Optional Application: What is the faith lesson being taught to the readers of Chronicles in 2 Chronicles 13:18, and how does it relate personally to you?

First Kings 15:3 gives Abijah a very low grade as king: he copied his father's sins, disregarded the Law of Moses, and his heart (desire, will, conscience) wasn't fully devoted to God. The Chronicler leaves out that failing grade. Instead, he focuses on one time when Abijah was devoted to God. He tells how Abijah was God's instrument of judgment on Jeroboam for his rebellion. The triumph of the covenant with David is most important to the Chronicler here.

9. In 13:4-12, what are the main points King Abijah makes in his speech to the king and people of the northern kingdom?

_____

_____

_____

_____

10. What does chapter 13 demonstrate about retribution for sin?

_____

_____

_____

_____

A covenant of salt (13:5). This term "denotes a permanent provision."[5] See also Leviticus 2:13; Numbers 18:19; 2 Kings 2:20.

They relied on the LORD, the God of their ancestors (13:18). The key to military success in Chronicles is to entrust one's whole self to the Lord. As He did for Abijah's ancestors (Abraham, Isaac, Jacob, David), God responds to total reliance.

---

11. What aspects of King Asa's reign are emphasized in chapter 14, and what is their significance?

_____

_____

_____

_____

_____

_____

12. Look at Asa's prayer in 14:11. What is his *praise*, what is his *confession*, and what is his *request*? And with what specific actions did God answer his prayer (see 14:12-15)?

_____

_____

_____

_____

_____

_____

Help us . . . we rely on you (14:11). Asa's prayer for help—and the same reliance we saw with Abijah—is the key to his military victory. At the dedication of the temple, Solomon had asked for exactly this response to prayer in wartime (see 6:34-35). The humility of these prayers contrasts sharply with what we read in inscriptions by kings of other nations in the

For Further Study: Compare 2 Chronicles 14:1-8 to the parallel account in 1 Kings 15:9-12.

For Thought and Discussion: As you reflect on King Asa's words in 2 Chronicles 14:7, what kinds of ideas and images come to mind when you think of someone who seeks God?

Optional Application: What is the faith lesson being taught to the readers of Chronicles in 2 Chronicles 14:7, and how does it relate personally to you?

ancient world, where they boast of their own prowess along with boasting of the strength of their gods.

13. What theological significance and spiritual instruction do you see in the words of the prophet Azariah to King Asa in 15:1-7?

_____

_____

_____

_____

The Spirit of God came on Azariah (15:1). This is what happens in Chronicles when God commissions someone to do some work, especially to speak in His Name (see 20:14; 24:20).[6]

For a long time Israel was without the true God. . . . But in their distress they turned to the LORD . . . and he was found by them (15:3-4). This cycle—abandoning God, experiencing distress from enemies or hardship, turning to the Lord, deliverance from distress—happens over and over from the book of Judges onward. God consistently helps those who wholeheartedly seek Him.[7]

14. Summarize how, in 15:8-19, King Asa and the people responded to the prophet Azariah's words.

_____

_____

_____

_____

A repulsive image for the worship of Asherah (15:16). "An Asherah pole . . . was a cultic symbol of the Canaanite fertility goddess Asherah in the form of a tree or tree trunk. The pole represented the tree of life in Canaanite religion."[8] Along with altars and sacred stones in general, Asherah poles were singled out repeatedly in the Law of Moses as idolatrous things that the Israelites were supposed to eliminate from the Promised Land (see Exodus 34:13; Deuteronomy 7:5; 16:21).

15. How would you summarize the closing years of King Asa's reign as described in chapter 16, and how do they impact the Chronicler's overall picture of this king?

_____

_____

_____

_____

Seer (16:7). A prophet, especially one who gets his message from God by seeing images in dreams or visions. The term was used more commonly in the time of Samuel (see 1 Samuel 9:9,19).[9]

16. What does chapter 16 demonstrate about retribution for sin?

_____

_____

_____

17. What timeless spiritual principles do you see emphasized in the details of Israel's history as recorded in 2 Chronicles 10–16?

_____

_____

For Further Study: Compare 2 Chronicles 16 to the parallel account in 1 Kings 15:16-24.

Optional Application: What personal encouragement and exhortation for your own walk with God do you see in the words of the prophet Hanani to King Asa in 2 Chronicles 16:9?

Optional Application: On the basis of God's truth revealed to you in this lesson, perhaps the Holy Spirit has helped you sense a new and higher reality in your life that God is inviting you to. If this is true for you, express in your own words the reality that you long for, and use it as a springboard for prayer.

18. In 2 Chronicles 10–16, what would you select as the key verse or passage — one that best captures or reflects the dynamics of what these chapters are all about?

19. List any lingering questions you have about 2 Chronicles 10–16.

For the group

You may want to focus your discussion for lesson 7 especially on some of the following issues, themes, and concepts (which are recognized as major over-all themes in 1 and 2 Chronicles). Which of these are dealt with in some way in chapters 10–16, and how are they further developed there?

- The meaning and significance of God's covenant relationship with His people
- God's nature, especially as revealed by how He acts in the details of His people's history
- The importance and meaning of worship
- For God's people, the continuity of the present with the past
- The importance of obedience to God's Word and His laws, and our personal responsibility in that regard
- How sin brings disaster and judgment from God

- God's continued blessings and grace for His people
- The future hope of God's people
- The unity of God's people
- God's sovereignty over His people's lives and history

The following numbered questions in lesson 7 may stimulate your best and most helpful discussion: 1, 4, 6, 13, 17, 18, and 19.

And again, remember to look at the "For Thought and Discussion" questions and discussion in the margins.

1. Andrew E. Hill, *1 & 2 Chronicles*, The NIV Application Commentary series, ed. Terry Much (Grand Rapids, MI: Zondervan, 2003), 455.
2. Hill, 456.
3. Hill, 461.
4. Hill, 461.
5. *ESV Study Bible* (Wheaton, IL: Crossway, 2008), at 2 Chronicles 13:5.
6. Hill, 471.
7. Hill, 471.
8. Hill, 473.
9. Hill, 475.

2 CHRONICLES 17–20

The Reign of Jehoshaphat

Chapters 17–20 center around Judah's King Jehoshaphat. David is the standard of ideal kingship, and Jehoshaphat (see 17:3), Hezekiah (see 29:2), and Josiah (see 34:2) are the only three kings of Judah whom the Chronicler compares to King David.[1] The writer of 1 Kings gives extensive coverage to the struggle between Elijah and King Ahab in the northern kingdom at this time, all of which the Chronicler omits. Instead, he devotes four chapters to Jehoshaphat, who gets only nine verses in 1 Kings.

1. In one sitting if possible, read attentively all of 2 Chronicles 17–20, taking notes and underlining or highlighting as you go. What impresses you overall as the key features and themes of this part of the book?

   _____

   _____

   _____

   _____

For Further Study: We read of Jehoshaphat that "his heart was devoted to the ways of the LORD" (2 Chronicles 17:6), at least in his early years. Related to this kind of heart-set, describe what spiritual instruction you see in the following passages: Deuteronomy 6:5; 11:13; 26:16; Jeremiah 29:13; Matthew 22:37; Romans 1:9; Ephesians 6:6.

For Further Study: Compare 2 Chronicles 18 to the parallel account in 1 Kings 22:1-40.

2. Summarize what happens in chapter 17 and what it reveals most about King Jehoshaphat and his heart and leadership.

   _____

   _____

   _____

   _____

3. Summarize what happens in chapter 18 and what it reveals most about King Jehoshaphat. In particular, how would you evaluate Jehoshaphat's responsibility in the joint defeat that Israel and Judah experienced in this chapter?

   _____

   _____

   _____

   _____

Someone drew his bow at random (18:33). This "random" arrow is from God and proves the prophet Micaiah correct (see 18:27).[2]

4. What particular significance do you see in the prophetic message given by the seer Jehu to King Jehoshaphat in 19:1-3?

   _____

   _____

   _____

   _____

5. How would you analyze the leadership King Jehoshaphat provides in the events described in 19:4-11?

   _____

   _____

_____

_____

Jehoshaphat lived in Jerusalem (19:4). He
    stopped traveling to the northern kingdom and
    ceased fighting alongside the north's wicked
    kings.[3] The words of Jehu the seer (see 19:1-3)
    seem to have gotten through to him.

He went out again among the people (19:4). This
    probably means Jehoshaphat again sent out his
    officials and Levites to teach the Law of Moses
    to the people (see 17:7-9). Jehu's warning may
    have motivated him here too.[4]

6. Summarize the crisis Jehoshaphat faces in
    chapter 20 and then write how you would ana-
    lyze the leadership he provides in facing this
    challenge.

_____

_____

_____

_____

_____

7. What are the most important aspects of King
    Jehoshaphat's prayer in 20:5-12? What points
    of praise does it include? What does the king
    "remind" God of? What confessions does he
    make? And what specifically does he ask God to
    do?

_____

_____

_____

_____

Optional Application: In what ways can King Jehoshaphat's prayer in 2 Chronicles 20:5-12 serve as a model for your own prayers?

8. Compare Jehoshaphat's prayer (see 20:5-12) with the prayer of David in 1 Chronicles 29:10-20.

_____

_____

_____

_____

Name (20:8-9). A reference to God's presence, the glory of the Lord.

In his prayer of 20:6-12, Jehoshaphat refers to God's covenant with Abraham to give his descendants the land (see 20:7); to God's covenant through Moses with the words about Ammon, Moab, and Mount Seir (Edom) at the time of Israel's entrance into the Promised Land (see 20:10-11); and to God's covenant with David in the reference to the temple (see 20:8-9).

9. In 20:14-17, what timeless significance do you see in the prophetic message given by Jahaziel in answer to the king's prayer?

_____

_____

_____

_____

Tomorrow (20:17). The situation is dire; the attackers are "only a day's march from Jerusalem!"[5]

_____

10. What significance and spiritual instruction do you see in the day's events—and the aftermath—as described in 20:20-30?

_____

_____

_____

_____

We do not know what to do, but our eyes are on you (20:12). An excellent expression of humility. Jehoshaphat humbles himself, prays, and seeks God wholeheartedly with his eyes on God.

The battle is not yours, but God's (20:15). The constantly repeated attitude toward warfare in the Old Testament. No other ancient nation would view warfare in this way. The New Testament takes this view of spiritual warfare.

Have faith in the LORD your God (20:20). We often think of the Old Testament as being about law as opposed to faith, but that is incorrect. Faith was as crucial in Old Testament times as it is today. Jehoshaphat taught the people the Law of Moses given by God (see 17:9) and he also exhorted them to have faith in God.

They began to sing and praise (20:22). This is the only place in the Bible where an army goes into battle singing praises to God.[6]

They entered Jerusalem and went to the temple of the LORD with harps and lyres and trumpets (20:28). The story of the war ends where it started, at the temple.[7]

Optional Application: In practical terms, how do you see Jehoshaphat's words to the people in 2 Chronicles 20:20 applying also to you?

For Further Study: What connections with the story in 2 Chronicles 20:1-30 do you see in Psalms 47, 96, and 98?

For Thought and Discussion: If you could go back in time to act as a royal adviser to King Jehoshaphat, what kind of counsel would you give him and how would you express it?

For Further Study: Compare 2 Chronicles 20:31-37 to the parallel account in 1 Kings 22:41-50.

11. What does the story in 20:1-30 reveal most about God's grace and power and about our true dependence on Him?

_____

_____

_____

_____

12. How would you summarize the closing years of King Jehoshaphat's reign as described in 20:31-37, and how do they impact the Chronicler's overall picture of this king?

_____

_____

_____

_____

_____

The high places, however, were not removed (20:33). Jehoshaphat did remove the Asherah poles (see 19:3) but did not obliterate the hilltop shrines where the poles had stood. Altars may have still stood there, because the people "had not set their hearts on the God of their ancestors" and continued to honor other gods in addition to the Lord.[8] Possibly Jehoshaphat would have had a rebellion on his hands if he had tried to destroy the hilltop shrines.

Eliezer . . . prophesied against Jehoshaphat (20:37). Even Jehoshaphat, one of the three best kings of the divided monarchy, gets a "mixed review."[9] Jehoshaphat's weakness seems to have been his alliances with the wicked kings of the northern kingdom.

13. What timeless spiritual principles do you see emphasized in the details of Israel's history as recorded in 2 Chronicles 17–20?

_____

_____

_____

_____

14. In 2 Chronicles 17–20, what would you select as the key verse or passage — one that best captures or reflects the dynamics of what these chapters are all about?

_____

_____

_____

_____

15. List any lingering questions you have about 2 Chronicles 17–20.

_____

_____

_____

_____

Optional Application: On the basis of God's truth revealed to you in this lesson, perhaps the Holy Spirit has helped you sense a new and higher reality in your life that God is inviting you to. If this is true for you, express in your own words the reality that you long for, and use it as a springboard for prayer.

For the group

You may want to focus your discussion for lesson 8 especially on some of the following issues, themes, and concepts (which are recognized as major overall themes in 1 and 2 Chronicles). Which of these are dealt with in some way in chapters 17–20, and how are they further developed there?

- The meaning and significance of God's covenant relationship with His people
- God's nature, especially as revealed by how He acts in the details of His people's history
- The importance and meaning of worship
- For God's people, the continuity of the present with the past

- The importance of obedience to God's Word and His laws, and our personal responsibility in that regard
- How sin brings disaster and judgment from God
- God's continued blessings and grace for His people
- The future hope of God's people
- The unity of God's people
- God's sovereignty over His people's lives and history

The following numbered questions in lesson 8 may stimulate your best and most helpful discussion: 1, 5, 6, 7, 9, 10, 11, 13, 14, and 15.

Look also at the question in the margin under the heading "For Thought and Discussion."

1. Andrew E. Hill, *1 & 2 Chronicles*, The NIV Application Commentary series, ed. Terry Much (Grand Rapids, MI: Zondervan, 2003), 477.
2. Hill, 484.
3. Hill, 485–486.
4. Hill, 485.
5. Hill, 491.
6. Hill, 491.
7. Hill, 492.
8. Hill, 485.
9. Hill, 477.

2 CHRONICLES 21–24

Further Crises

1. In one sitting if possible, read attentively all of 2 Chronicles 21–24, taking notes and underlining or highlighting as you go. What impresses you overall as the key features and themes of this part of the book?

_____

_____

_____

_____

For Further Study: Compare 2 Chronicles 21:1-11 to the parallel account in 2 Kings 8:16-22.

2. From all you see in chapter 21, what is it the Lord most wants His people to remember about King Jehoram?

_____

_____

_____

_____

Put all his brothers to the sword (21:4). This was an all-too-common practice in nations where kings had multiple wives. The brothers were often half-brothers and rivals for the throne.

For Further Study:
Compare 2 Chronicles
21:18-20 to the paral-
lel account in 2 Kings
8:23-24.

**Optional
Application:** In
2 Chronicles 21:20,
notice the response
to King Jehoram's
death. What would
you say is the best
way for you to pre-
vent the same kind
of response to *your*
death?

Some considerable jockeying for power went
on when a king was dying and his various sons
competed to succeed him. The victor often
dispatched the losers to avoid palace coups later
on. The fact that a king of Judah did this shows
how much Jehoram was walking in the ways of
the kings of the northern kingdom (see 21:6)
rather than the ways of the Lord.

A lamp for him and his descendants forever
(21:7). A picture of persistent light in dark days.
The Chronicler will go on to highlight how
close the lamp of David got to being snuffed out
through war and murder (see 21:4,17; 22:10).
The lamp was preserved by God's grace, but
Jehoram paid the price of his wickedness in con-
stant battles with subject nations and neighbors
(see 21:10-20).[1]

God's faithfulness to His promise to David
is a continuing theme in the Bible.[2] The Chronicler traces the theme until the exile. For the
rest of the Old Testament period the question
is, when will a descendant of David become
king of Israel again? Who will he be? The Gos-
pels proclaim Jesus as that King and show how
enemies try to kill Him and His family even
when He is a baby (see Matthew 2:13-18). After
Jesus' resurrection and on through the book of
Revelation, the Enemy continues to try to put
out His lamp and eliminate His spiritual family.

3. What is the substance and significance of
Elijah's letter to Jehoram in 21:12-15?

_____

_____

_____

_____

4. Summarize what happens in chapter 22, and
explain its significance. What human actions
in this chapter do you think were most pleasing
to God? And which do you think were most dis-
pleasing to Him?

_____

For Further Study:
Compare 2 Chronicles 22:1-9 to the parallel account in 2 Kings 8:25-29; 9:15-16,27-28; 10:12-14.

For Further Study:
Compare 2 Chronicles 22:10-12 to the parallel account in 2 Kings 11:1-3.

_____

_____

_____

_____

_____

5. From all you see in chapter 22, what is it the Lord most wants His people to remember about King Ahaziah?

_____

_____

_____

_____

_____

_____

Athaliah, a granddaughter of Omri (22:2). A daughter of Ahab and Jezebel of the northern kingdom. Jehoshaphat made a foolish alliance with Ahab (see 18:1) and narrowly escaped trouble from it during his lifetime. But the trouble came later. His son Jehoram walked in the ways of Ahab's family and married a daughter of Ahab: Athaliah. Her loyalties were with the north and with gods other than the Lord. She decided to destroy Judah's royal family (see 22:10). If she had succeeded, the lamp of David would have gone out; the line of the Messiah would have ended.

Jehosheba . . . took Joash son of Ahaziah and stole him away. . . . She hid the child from Athaliah (22:11). Like Moses and Samuel before him and Jesus after him, Joash is a "vulnerable [infant] through whom God achieves his covenant purposes (see Exodus 2:1-10; 1 Samuel 1:24-28; Matthew 2:13-23)."[3]

93

6. In chapter 23, summarize the events that brought young Joash to the throne, and explain their significance.

_____

_____

_____

_____

_____

_____

The first stage of Jehoiada's plan involves assembling a coalition of military leaders, religious leaders (Levites), and community leaders (heads of families, see 23:1-3). Next, he makes sure that all of them — including the Levites — are armed, and he positions them at strategic places in and around the temple (see 23:3-7). With Joash thus well defended, he presents him to be recognized as the rightful king (see 23:8-11).[4]

Standing by his pillar at the entrance (23:13). Beside one of the two bronze pillars was apparently the customary place where the king used to stand before Athaliah took over (see 2 Kings 11:14).[5]

Jehoiada then made a covenant that he, the people and the king would be the LORD's people. All the people went to the temple of Baal and tore it down. . . . Then Jehoiada placed the oversight of the temple of the LORD in the hands of the Levitical priests (23:16-18). "For the Chronicler, the restoration of proper temple worship is no less important than the reestablishment of Davidic kingship in Judah."[6]

All the people of the land rejoiced (23:21). The Chronicler often speaks of the people rejoicing when God's will is again being obeyed (see 1 Chronicles 29:9; 2 Chronicles 15:15; 29:36).[7]

And the city was calm (23:21). Again, the Chronicler often describes periods of time when the people are obeying God's will in terms like "the city was calm," "the land was quiet" (see 1 Chronicles 4:40; 22:9; 2 Chronicles 14:4-5).[8] Rest from strife is the Chronicler's ideal condition for God's people and a sign of His blessing.

For Further Study:
Compare 2 Chronicles 23 to the parallel account in 2 Kings 11:4-20.

For Further Study:
Compare 2 Chronicles 24:1-14 to the parallel account in 2 Kings 11:21–12:1.

7. From what you see in chapter 23, how would you summarize the character strengths and leadership capabilities of Jehoiada the priest?

_____

_____

_____

8. What are the most important decisions and choices made in chapter 24, and how would you analyze each one?

_____

_____

_____

_____

_____

9. In 24:20, what did the Spirit of God most want the people to understand in His words to them through the prophet Zechariah?

_____

_____

_____

_____

For Further Study: Compare 2 Chronicles 24:23-27 to the parallel account in 2 Kings 12:17-21.

For Thought and Discussion: If you could go back in time to act as a royal adviser to King Joash, what kind of counsel would you give him and how would you express it?

For Thought and Discussion: What would you say are the most useful and important lessons to learn from the life of Joash?

Optional Application: On the basis of God's truth revealed to you in this lesson, perhaps the Holy Spirit has helped you sense a new and higher reality in your life that God is inviting you to. If this is true for you, express in your own words the reality that you long for, and use it as a springboard for prayer.

Old and full of years (24:15). Compare the description of David in 1 Chronicles 23:1. This is a rare mention in Chronicles of the long and blessed life of someone who wasn't a king. He was a priest who served as regent, so he was buried with the kings and the Chronicler compares him to David with these words. After his death Joash's reign changed dramatically.

In the courtyard of the LORD's temple (24:21). The murder occurs in the very place where Zechariah and his brothers had joined in crowning Joash king (see 23:11).[9]

Who said as he lay dying, "May the LORD see this and call you to account" (24:22). Zechariah is asking God to act in accord with His justice.[10]

10. From all you see in chapter 24, what is it the Lord most wants His people to remember about King Joash?

_____

_____

_____

_____

11. What timeless spiritual principles do you see emphasized in the details of Israel's history as recorded in 2 Chronicles 21–24?

_____

_____

_____

_____

12. In 2 Chronicles 21–24, what would you select as the key verse or passage—one that best captures or reflects the dynamics of what these chapters are all about?

_____

_____

_____

_____

_____

13. List any lingering questions you have about
    2 Chronicles 21–24.

_____

_____

_____

_____

For the group

You may want to focus your discussion for lesson 9
especially on some of the following issues, themes,
and concepts (which are recognized as major overall themes in 1 and 2 Chronicles). Which of these
are dealt with in some way in chapters 21–24, and
how are they further developed there?

* The meaning and significance of God's cov-
  enant relationship with His people
* God's nature, especially as revealed by how He
  acts in the details of His people's history
* The importance and meaning of worship
* For God's people, the continuity of the present
  with the past
* The importance of obedience to God's Word and
  His laws, and our personal responsibility in that
  regard
* How sin brings disaster and judgment from God
* God's continued blessings and grace for His
  people
* The future hope of God's people
* The unity of God's people
* God's sovereignty over His people's lives and
  history

    The following numbered questions in lesson 9
may stimulate your best and most helpful discussion: 1, 2, 4, 6, 7, 8, 11, 12, and 13.
    Remember to look also at the "For Thought
and Discussion" questions in the margin.

1. *ESV Study Bible* (Wheaton, IL: Crossway, 2008), at 2 Chronicles 21:7.
2. Andrew E. Hill, *1 & 2 Chronicles*, The NIV Application Commentary series, ed. Terry Much (Grand Rapids, MI: Zondervan, 2003), 514.
3. Hill, 522.
4. Hill, 522.
5. Hill, 523.
6. Hill, 524.
7. Hill, 525.
8. Hill, 525.
9. Hill, 541.
10. Hill, 541.

Lesson Ten

2 CHRONICLES 25–28

Further Decline

1. In one sitting if possible, read attentively all of 2 Chronicles 25–28, taking notes and underlining or highlighting as you go. What impresses you overall as the key features and themes of this part of the book?

_____

_____

_____

_____

The accounts of Amaziah (chapter 25) and Uzziah (chapter 26) echo the account of Joash (chapter 24) in several ways. First, in each case the king started out obeying the covenant with God but fell away. Joash did well when Jehoiada was alive but then "abandoned . . . the Lord . . . and worshiped . . . idols" (24:18). Amaziah, likewise, acted in accord with the Law (see 25:4) and heeded a prophet (see 25:7-10) but later "turned away from following the Lord" (25:27). And Uzziah "sought God during the days of Zechariah" (26:5) but later "was unfaithful to the Lord his God" (26:16).

Predictably, in each case the king was

(continued on page 100)

(continued from page 99)
successful in governing and warfare when he was obedient to God but faced defeat when he committed idolatry.

Finally, each king rejected wise counsel and suffered for it (see 24:20-21; 25:15-16; 26:18-19). This follows a theme from Proverbs about wisdom: "the way of fools seems right to them, but the wise listen to advice" (Proverbs 12:15).[1]

2. From all you see in chapter 25, what is it the Lord most wants His people to remember about King Amaziah?

_____

_____

_____

_____

"By this point in our progress through 2 Chronicles, it is obvious that the main motif is that a good man is hard to find. Even with the good kings, there is a fly in the ointment—a flaw in the royal throne."[2]

3. What are the most important decisions and choices Amaziah made in chapter 25, and how would you analyze each one?

_____

_____

_____

_____

_____

_____

He . . . acted in accordance with what is written in the Law (25:4). In this case, obeying the Law was also good political policy. Executing his father's murderers strengthened his own legitimacy as rightful king, not as a co-conspirator against his father.

Man of God (25:7). A term for a prophet. By not naming him, the Chronicler emphasizes the message not the messenger.[3]

But what about the hundred talents I paid for these Israelite troops? (25:9). A hundred talents was a huge amount of money: 3.75 tons of silver, with a buying power much higher then than now. But God's help was priceless.[4]

For Further Study:
Compare 2 Chronicles 25 to the parallel account in 2 Kings 14:1-20.

What value is there in reading these often-depressing stories of wayward kings? First, we see "God's patience with fallen humanity" and are motivated to be grateful for His patience with us in our fallenness. Second, we are warned not to try to serve other "gods" (money, success, people's opinion) alongside the Lord (see Matthew 6:24; 1 Corinthians 10:11-13). Third, we are reminded that what counts with God is our hearts (see Romans 2:28), not membership in the right church or family.[5]

4. From all you see in chapter 26, what is it the Lord most wants His people to remember about King Uzziah?

_____

_____

_____

_____

For Further Study:
Compare 2 Chronicles
26:1-15 to the paral-
lel account in 2 Kings
14:21-22; 15:1-7.

For Thought and
Discussion: If you
could go back in
time to act as a
royal adviser to King
Uzziah, what kind of
counsel would you
give him and how
would you express it?

5. How would you analyze the strengths and
   weaknesses of King Uzziah as you observe him
   in chapter 26?

_____

_____

_____

_____

*He did what was right in the eyes of the LORD,
just as his father Amaziah had done* (26:4).
"We should read that as code that means
Uzziah was a combination of good and bad [like
Amaziah, who ended up as an idolater]. . . .
By now . . . we should have picked up on the
Chronicler's distinctive way of conducting his
history."[6] He doesn't always spell out the irony
he expects his readers to pick up on.

*Uzziah had a well-trained army, ready to go out
by divisions. . . . Uzziah provided shields,
spears, helmets, coats of armor, bows and
slingstones for the entire army* (26:11,14).
In 1 Chronicles 27:1 we read that David's army
was made up of citizen soldiers who served
one month per year and otherwise had peace-
time jobs. These citizen soldiers provided their
own modest weaponry (see Judges 20:16-17;
1 Chronicles 12:2,8,24) and were obliged to
trust God in any conflict they faced. Now,
though, Uzziah has formed a standing army
of professionals and is providing them with
armaments paid for by taxes. This is an army
like the surrounding nations have, not an army
that relies on God for its victories.

*After Uzziah became powerful, his pride led to
his downfall* (26:16). His pride in his success
causes his failure.[7]

*While he was raging at the priests . . . before
the incense altar* (26:19). Uzziah was warned
that he had no business being in the Holy
Place before the incense altar, much less raging at God's servants in that sacred place. His

disrespect for God's servants in His holy pre-
cinct indicates profound disrespect for God.[8]
He's acting as if God's holiness is just an idea
instead of a potent reality.

For Further Study:
Compare 2 Chronicles
27:1-9 to the parallel
account in 2 Kings
15:32-38.

*Buried near them in a cemetery . . . for people
said, "He had leprosy"* (26:23). Leprosy made
him ritually unclean (see Leviticus 13) and
made anyone he touched unclean, so he had to
be kept away from other people and out of the
temple during his lifetime. Because it caused
uncleanness, leprosy had a stigma that Uzziah
bore even to the grave.

6. From all you see in chapter 27, what is it the
Lord most wants His people to remember about
King Jotham?

_____

_____

_____

_____

7. What particular significance do you see in the
statement made about King Jotham in 27:6?

_____

_____

_____

_____

_____

He walked steadfastly before the LORD his God
(27:6). Literally, "he ordered his ways before the
Lord his God" (ESV). An unusual expression that
is equivalent to "doing what was good and right
and faithful before the LORD his God" (31:20).
His life was well ordered, with the right priorities in the right order consistently.

For Thought and Discussion: How many favorable things can you find written about King Ahaz in chapter 28?

For Further Study: Compare 2 Chronicles 28 to the parallel account in 2 Kings 16:1-12.

8. From all you see in chapter 28, what is it the Lord most wants His people to remember about King Ahaz?

_____

_____

_____

_____

9. In 28:9-11, what did the Lord most want His people to understand in His words to them through the prophet Oded?

_____

_____

_____

_____

10. What does chapter 28 demonstrate about retribution for sin?

_____

_____

_____

_____

The men . . . took the prisoners, and . . . they clothed all who were naked. They provided them with clothes and sandals, food and drink, and healing balm. All those who were weak they put on donkeys. So they took them back to their fellow Israelites at Jericho, the City of Palms (28:15). A complete reversal of what was normally done with prisoners. In His story of the Good Samaritan (see Luke 10:25-37), Jesus may have deliberately echoed this story in Chronicles about enemy Samaritans providing men of Judah with clothing, food, and healing oil.[9]

11. What timeless spiritual principles do you see emphasized in the details of Israel's history as recorded in 2 Chronicles 25–28?

_____

_____

_____

_____

Optional Application: On the basis of God's truth revealed to you in this lesson, perhaps the Holy Spirit has helped you sense a new and higher reality in your life that God is inviting you to. If this is true for you, express in your own words the reality that you long for, and use it as a springboard for prayer.

12. In 2 Chronicles 25–28, what would you select as the key verse or passage—one that best captures or reflects the dynamics of what these chapters are all about?

_____

_____

_____

_____

13. List any lingering questions you have about 2 Chronicles 25–28.

_____

_____

_____

_____

For the group

You may want to focus your discussion for lesson 10 especially on some of the following issues, themes, and concepts (which are recognized as major overall themes in 1 and 2 Chronicles). Which of these are dealt with in some way in chapters 25–28, and how are they further developed there?

- The meaning and significance of God's covenant relationship with His people
- God's nature, especially as revealed by how He acts in the details of His people's history
- The importance and meaning of worship

- For God's people, the continuity of the present with the past
- The importance of obedience to God's Word and His laws, and our personal responsibility in that regard
- How sin brings disaster and judgment from God
- God's continued blessings and grace for His people
- The future hope of God's people
- The unity of God's people
- God's sovereignty over His people's lives and history

The following numbered questions in lesson 10 may stimulate your best and most helpful discussion: 1, 4, 5, 11, 12, and 13.

Remember to look also at the "For Thought and Discussion" questions in the margins.

1. Andrew E. Hill, *1 & 2 Chronicles*, The NIV Application Commentary series, ed. Terry Much (Grand Rapids, MI: Zondervan, 2003), 537–538.
2. Leland Ryken and Philip Graham Ryken, eds., *The Literary Study Bible* (Wheaton, IL: Crossway, 2007), at 1 Chronicles 25.
3. Hill, 544–545.
4. Hill, 545.
5. M. J. Selman, in Hill, 549.
6. Ryken and Ryken, at 1 Chronicles 26.
7. Hill, 551.
8. Hill, 552.
9. Hill, 576.

2 CHRONICLES 29–32

The Reign of Hezekiah

1. In one sitting if possible, read attentively all of 2 Chronicles 29–32, taking notes and underlining or highlighting as you go. What impresses you overall as the key features and themes of this part of the book?

_____

_____

_____

_____

For Further Study: Compare 2 Chronicles 29:1-2 to the parallel account in 2 Kings 18:1-8.

2. Summarize the most significant things we see in chapter 29 regarding King Hezekiah's temple reforms.

_____

_____

_____

_____

He opened the doors of the temple of the LORD (29:3). Opening the doors is a powerful image of inviting the people to turn away from their idols and come in again to the Lord's temple,

Optional Application: In 2 Chronicles 29:11, Hezekiah tells the priests and Levites, "The LORD has chosen you to stand before him and serve him, to minister before him." As fully as you can explain it, what has God chosen *you* for?

Optional Application: Look again at 2 Chronicles 29:36. What accomplishments by God can the people of your church find to rejoice about today?

where they could worship as they were created to worship.[1]

An object of dread and horror and scorn (29:8). Jeremiah said God's anger expressed through the Babylonian exile made Judah an object of "horror and scorn" (Jeremiah 25:9,18).[2] The Chronicler chooses these same words for Hezekiah. He even speaks of "captivity" in 2 Chronicles 29:9. Hezekiah's speech is thus something the Chronicler's first readers could take to heart.

3. In 29:10, what is the significance of the reason Hezekiah gives for his actions?

_____

_____

_____

_____

_____

I intend to make a covenant with the LORD (29:10). Like Moses, Hezekiah is making a covenant with the Lord on behalf of the people. He's taking them back to the birth of their nation at Mount Sinai. He's asking them to start anew with freshly focused priorities.[3]

The Levites had been more conscientious in consecrating themselves than the priests had been (29:34). After sixteen years, when the temple was abandoned under King Ahaz, and still more years, when the people were practicing idolatry on the side, the priests have become lax. They don't take the Lord's holiness seriously. They don't think He would really strike someone with leprosy or even strike them dead, as had happened centuries earlier in the time of David (see 1 Chronicles 13:10).

4. What is the special significance of the summary statement given in 29:36?

_____

_____

_____

_____

5. Summarize the most significant things we see in chapter 30 regarding King Hezekiah's leadership in celebrating the Passover.

_____

_____

_____

_____

6. Summarize the main points in King Hezekiah's letter to all the people as recorded in 30:6-9. What theological significance and spiritual instruction do you see here?

_____

_____

_____

_____

_____

Throughout Israel and Judah (30:6). Hezekiah reaches out even to the people of the northern kingdom, recalling a hope for the unity of "all Israel."

Return to the Lord . . . that he may return to you (30:6). A prophetic call, like Ezekiel's "turn to God and live" (see Ezekiel 18:23,32).[4] "Return" also recalls 2 Chronicles 7:14, "turn from their wicked ways." Turning back to the Lord, changing direction to walk toward Him, is the fundamental movement He calls for, and it's never too late. God can't return to us if we won't return to Him.

For Further Study:
As you reflect on
the portrait of God's
people given in the
Passover celebra-
tion described in
2 Chronicles 30, com-
pare this to the New
Testament portrayal
of God's people in
these passages: Luke
2:32; Acts 9:15; 11:1,18;
Galatians 3:14,29;
4:28; 6:16; Ephesians
2:11-22; 3:6. What con-
nections do you see?

**Optional
Application:**
Considering
Hezekiah's example
of intercession in
2 Chronicles 30:18-19,
who among those
who might be "not
clean" in some way is
the Spirit of God lead-
ing you to pray for?

7. What various responses to Hezekiah's invitation
   are mentioned in 30:10-12, and what does this
   reveal about the people?

   _____

   _____

   _____

   _____

   _____

   _____

---

*Many in the crowd had not consecrated them-
selves . . . yet they ate the Passover, con-
trary to what was written. But Hezekiah
prayed for them, saying, "May the LORD,
who is good, pardon everyone who sets their
heart on seeking God . . . even if they are
not clean according to the rules of the sanc-
tuary"* (30:17-19). As much as he revels in the
details of temple worship and the proper way to
treat the holy things of a holy God, the Chronicler puts in this prayer to make clear that
"intent of heart and acts of repentance, when
combined with intercessory prayer, override the
letter of the law" in worship.[5]

Healed the people (30:20). Healed their relation-
ships with God and one another. They are now
keeping their covenant with God, and members
of the northern and southern kingdoms are
worshiping together.[6]

God heard them (30:27). The Chronicler is telling
his own generation that right worship leads to
answered prayer.[7]

8. Summarize the most significant things we see
   in chapter 31 regarding King Hezekiah's further
   reforms.

   _____

   _____

9. How would you describe the spiritual health of God's people as indicated in chapter 31?

10. What particular spiritual instruction do you see for God's people today in the example of Hezekiah as stated in 31:20-21?

He sought his God and worked wholeheartedly (31:21). The key to prosperity for the Chronicler. Note once again the reference to the heart.

---

11. In chapter 32, what are the most significant elements in the narrative about the Assyrian threat to Israel, and what is their theological significance?

Optional Application: Reflect again on Hezekiah's example as summarized in 2 Chronicles 31:20-21. How is God using these words to summon you to greater excellence, wholeheartedness, and diligence in your service to Him? How does He want you to respond?

For Further Study: Compare 2 Chronicles 32:1-23 to the parallel accounts in 2 Kings 18:13–19:37 and Isaiah 36:1–38:2.

Optional Application: What is the faith lesson being taught to the readers of Chronicles in 2 Chronicles 32:20-21, and how does it relate personally to you?

Sennacherib invaded Judah in 701 BC (see 2 Kings 18:13). It was a huge event in Judah's history, and the Chronicler's readers would have been familiar with the story from 2 Kings 18–19 and Isaiah 36–37. So the Chronicler gives an abridged account.

All that Hezekiah had so faithfully done (32:1). The renewal of proper temple worship described in chapters 30–31. These acts were why the Lord had mercy on Judah.[8]

There is a greater power with us than with him (32:7). A renewal of the old attitude toward military matters, after Uzziah's detour into trusting in a professional army. No professional army fielded by Judah could have withstood Assyria anyway.

So the LORD saved Hezekiah and the people of Jerusalem (32:22). "The Chronicler understands the simple truth that people are people, nothing more, and that God is God, nothing less."[9]

12. How would you summarize the closing years of King Hezekiah's reign as described in 32:24-33, and how do they impact the Chronicler's overall picture of this king?

_____

_____

_____

_____

_____

_____

13. In your own words, how would you describe the stages in Hezekiah's relationship with God as revealed in 32:25-26?

_____

_____

_____

_____

Optional Application: Think again about the way God tested Hezekiah's heart, as mentioned in 2 Chronicles 32:31. What kind of testing is God continuing to take you through? What kinds of things in your heart are being exposed by this testing? What aspects of the goodness and grace of God do you recognize in this process?

But . . . God left him to test him and to know everything that was in his heart (32:31). God didn't test Hezekiah because God was in suspense about how wholehearted Hezekiah's faith was. He tested him because the test gave Hezekiah a chance to know his own heart, to grow wiser with the knowledge, and to respond in faith fueled by that wisdom.[10]

For Thought and Discussion: If you could go back in time to act as a royal adviser to King Hezekiah, what kind of counsel would you give him and how would you express it?

14. From all you see in chapters 29–32, what is it the Lord most wants His people to remember about King Hezekiah?

_____

_____

_____

_____

For Further Study: Compare 2 Chronicles 32:24-33 to the parallel account in 2 Kings 20.

15. What timeless spiritual principles do you see emphasized in the details of Israel's history as recorded in 2 Chronicles 29–32?

_____

_____

_____

_____

16. In 2 Chronicles 29–32, what would you select as the key verse or passage — one that best captures or reflects the dynamics of what these chapters are all about?

_____

_____

17. List any lingering questions you have about 2 Chronicles 29–32.

For the group

You may want to focus your discussion for lesson 11 especially on some of the following issues, themes, and concepts (which are recognized as major overall themes in 1 and 2 Chronicles). Which of these are dealt with in some way in chapters 29–32, and how are they further developed there?

- The meaning and significance of God's covenant relationship with His people
- God's nature, especially as revealed by how He acts in the details of His people's history
- The importance and meaning of worship
- For God's people, the continuity of the present with the past
- The importance of obedience to God's Word and His laws, and our personal responsibility in that regard
- How sin brings disaster and judgment from God
- God's continued blessings and grace for His people
- The future hope of God's people
- The unity of God's people
- God's sovereignty over His people's lives and history

The following numbered questions in lesson 11 may stimulate your best and most helpful discussion: 1, 2, 5, 10, 11, 12, 13, 15, 16, and 17.

Remember to look also at the "For Thought and Discussion" question in the margin.

1. Andrew E. Hill, *1 & 2 Chronicles*, The NIV Application Commentary series, ed. Terry Much (Grand Rapids, MI: Zondervan, 2003), 598.
2. Hill, 580.
3. Hill, 580, 598.
4. Hill, 599.
5. Hill, 587.
6. Hill, 587.
7. Hill, 588.
8. Hill, 592.
9. Hill, 600.
10. Hill, 596.

Lesson Twelve

2 CHRONICLES 33-36

The Kingdom's Fall

1. In one sitting if possible, read attentively all of 2 Chronicles 33–36, taking notes and underlining or highlighting as you go. What impresses you overall as the key features and themes of this final part of the Chronicles?

_____

_____

_____

_____

2. From all you see in 2 Chronicles 33:1-20, what is it the Lord most wants His people to remember about King Manasseh?

_____

_____

_____

_____

For Further Study:
Compare 2 Chronicles 33 to the parallel account in 2 Kings 21.

Manasseh ruled fifty-five years — longer than any other king of Judah or Israel. But the Chronicler gives him only twenty verses because there is only a brief, edifying story to tell about him. He was the reverse of Amaziah and Uzziah — he started out evil but changed course when the Lord disciplined him.

God had said . . . "In this temple . . . I will put my Name forever" (33:7). See 2 Chronicles 7:16.

Sought the favor (33:12). Literally, "softened the face." This is said of Moses, Hezekiah, and Daniel in their prayers (see Exodus 32:11; Jeremiah 26:19; Daniel 9:13). It is an appeal for mercy.[1] That God gave mercy to such a wicked king is a testament to God's grace.

Humbled himself greatly . . . prayed (33:12-13). An echo of 7:14. Manasseh didn't just pray this in desperation and then fall away when he was out of captivity. He remained faithful even after he was freed from exile in Babylon. A good example for the Chroniclers' readers.

Manasseh's reforms described in 2 Chronicles 33:14-17 correspond to the healing of the land promised in 7:14.[2] But the people continued to worship on the high places (see 33:17), so it's not clear how deep his reforms ran. Also, his son abandoned them.

3. From all you see in 33:21-25, what is it the Lord most wants His people to remember about King Amon?

_____

_____

_____

_____

Somehow, the idols Manasseh made survived his reforms (see 33:22). This adds another question about the depth of his reforms. Whatever the case, his son's two-year reign was notable only for Amon's refusal to humble himself, pray, and seek God's face (see 33:23).

For Further Study:
Compare 2 Chronicles 34 to the parallel account in 2 Kings 22:1–23:20.

4. What does chapter 33 demonstrate about retribution for sin?

_____

_____

_____

_____

5. What does chapter 33 reveal about the power of repentance?

_____

_____

_____

6. Look at the description of Josiah's relationship with God in the first half of 2 Chronicles 34:3. How do you see this commitment reflected in the further events of chapters 34 and 35?

_____

_____

_____

_____

7. Summarize what happens in 34:1-22, and explain its significance.

_____

_____

_____

Optional Application: What personal encouragement and exhortation for your own walk with God do you see in the words of the prophet Huldah to King Josiah in 2 Chronicles 34:27?

The Book of the Law of the LORD that had been given through Moses (34:14). The scroll is called "the Book of the Law" in 34:15 and "the Book of the Covenant" in 34:30. Most scholars think it was the book of Deuteronomy. It was lost either because it was hidden during an invasion threat (such as the Assyrians in the time of Hezekiah), or because it was rejected during the time of one of the wicked kings, or because lax priests put it away at some point.[3]

The prophet Huldah (34:22). Miriam, Deborah, and Huldah are the only Old Testament women named as prophets (see Exodus 15:20; Judges 4:4). Huldah must have been highly respected, because she is the person the officials went to when the king asked them to find someone with the authority to speak about the Book of the Law. Her interpretation of the book is taken as an authoritative word from God.[4]

8. In 34:22-28, what did the Lord most want the king and the people to understand in His words to them through Huldah the prophet?

9. From what you see in 34:29-33, summarize the response of King Josiah and the people to Huldah's prophetic message.

_____

_____

*He had everyone in Jerusalem and Benjamin
pledge themselves to it* (34:32). The people
evidently have to be ordered to pledge themselves to keep the covenant. Their attitude is
much different from the attitude reflected in
the chapters on Hezekiah. They obey during
Josiah's lifetime but fall away as soon as he dies
(see 2 Chronicles 36:8,14; Jeremiah 3:10).[5]

10. In 35:1-19, what theological significance and
    spiritual instruction do you see in the narrative
    regarding the reinstitution of the Passover?

_____

_____

_____

_____

*He . . . encouraged them in the service of the
LORD's temple* (35:2). He does his best to
encourage the priests, as Hezekiah did (see
30:22), but he can do only so much with people
who are fundamentally not as interested in the
Lord as he is.

11. How would you summarize the closing years
    of King Josiah's reign as described in 35:20-27,
    and how do they impact the Chronicler's overall
    picture of this king?

_____

_____

_____

_____

For Further Study:
Compare 2 Chronicles 35 to the parallel account in 2 Kings 23:21-30.

For Thought and Discussion: If you could go back in time to act as a royal adviser to King Josiah, what kind of counsel would you give him and how would you express it?

_____

_____

Necho king of Egypt went up to fight at Carchemish on the Euphrates (35:20). Almost a century has passed since the Assyrians besieged Jerusalem in Hezekiah's day (see 32:1-23). Assyria's vast power is waning, and Babylonia is about to swallow it. Babylonia's onslaught has forced a desperate Assyrian king to set up a temporary government at Carchemish. Necho of Egypt wants to help his Assyrian allies, and to get to Carchemish he has to march his army through Judah. Josiah wants to stop the Egyptians from raping and plundering their way through his country. So Josiah attacks the Egyptians.

He would not listen to what Necho had said at God's command (35:22). The Chronicler doesn't say how Josiah could have known that the king of Egypt was speaking for God. Somehow, either directly or through a prophet, God's Spirit gave Josiah the information he needed, but he ignored it.

2 Chronicles 36: Historical Background

In chapter 36, the Chronicler briefly summarizes a history that his readers know all too well. He leaves it to the prophets and Lamentations to tell the full story of Judah's death spiral.

Josiah attacked Necho, and Necho won. Necho thus took control of the whole of the Promised Land, which he hadn't set out to do. Assyria fell to Babylonia anyway, but Necho of Egypt was still in charge of Judah. Judah never again became a self-governing nation.

Josiah's son Jehoahaz only reigned three months before he was taken captive to Egypt. Necho put Jehoahaz's brother Jehoiakim on the throne as a puppet king. Judah remained a vassal of Egypt for seven years. Then the Babylonians defeated Egypt in two battles, and Judah became a vassal of Babylonia in 603 BC.

King Nebuchadnezzar of Babylon was distracted for a couple of years in 601-598 BC, and Judah temporarily asserted her freedom. But then in 598, Nebuchadnezzar came down hard on Judah, took captives to Babylon, and made Zedekiah a puppet king.

Against the advice of the prophet Jeremiah, Zedekiah finally went along with a revolt against Babylon in 589. Nebuchadnezzar besieged Jerusalem in 588 and obliterated the city in 587. Solomon's glorious temple was demolished and the population deported.

For Further Study:
Compare 2 Chronicles 36:1-21 to the parallel account in 2 Kings 23:21–25:21.

For Further Study:
Compare 2 Chronicles 36:22-23 to the parallel account in Ezra 1:1-3.

12. Summarize all that happens in chapter 36, and explain its significance.

_____

_____

_____

_____

_____

_____

Optional Application: On the basis of God's truth revealed to you in this lesson, perhaps the Holy Spirit has helped you sense a new and higher reality in your life that God is inviting you to. If this is true for you, express in your own words the reality that you long for, and use it as a springboard for prayer.

In fulfillment of the word of the Lord spoken by Jeremiah (36:21). See Jeremiah 1:1; 25:11; 27:22; 29:10; 40:1. See also Daniel 9:2; Zechariah 1:12; 7:5. The Chronicler wants his readers to remember that these terrible events were not out of God's control, but were precisely promised by God and then fulfilled.

The last two verses of Chronicles are copied from the first three verses of Ezra. By repeating the decree of King Cyrus of Persia, this addition splices the two books together. The splice makes the sad end of Chronicles transition smoothly to the rebuilding of the Jerusalem temple in Ezra.[6]

13. What timeless spiritual principles do you see emphasized in the details of Israel's history as recorded in 2 Chronicles 33–36?

_____

_____

_____

_____

14. In 2 Chronicles 33–36, what would you select as the key verse or passage — one that best captures or reflects the dynamics of what these chapters are all about?

_____

_____

_____

_____

15. List any lingering questions you have about 2 Chronicles 33–36.

_____

_____

_____

_____

Reviewing 1 and 2 Chronicles

16. Although the two books of Chronicles cover much of the history found also in 1 and 2 Kings, what major differences do you see in the themes and messages of these two sets of books?

_____

_____

_____

_____

17. In Isaiah 55:10-11, God reminds us that in the same way He sends rain and snow from the sky to water the earth and nurture life, so also He sends His words to accomplish specific purposes. What would you suggest are God's primary purposes for the message of 1 and 2 Chronicles in the lives of His people today?

_____

_____

_____

_____

_____

18. Recall the guidelines given for our thought-life in Philippians 4:8 — "Whatever is true, whatever is noble, whatever is right, whatever is pure, whatever is lovely, whatever is admirable — if anything is excellent or praiseworthy — think about such things." As you

Optional Application: Which verses in 1 and 2 Chronicles would be most helpful for you to memorize so you have them always available in your mind and heart for the Holy Spirit to use?

reflect on all you've read in the books of 1 and 2 Chronicles, what stands out to you as being particularly *true*, or *noble*, or *right*, or *pure*, or *lovely*, or *admirable*, or *excellent*, or *praise-worthy* — and therefore well worth thinking more about?

_____

_____

_____

19. Considering that all of Scripture testifies ultimately of Christ, where does Jesus come most into focus for you in these books?

_____

_____

_____

20. In your understanding, what are the strongest ways in which 1 and 2 Chronicles point us to mankind's need for Jesus and what He accomplished in His death and resurrection?

_____

_____

_____

21. Recall Paul's reminder that the Old Testament Scriptures can give us patience and perseverance on one hand as well as comfort and encouragement on the other (see Romans 15:4). In your own life, how do you see the books of 1 and 2 Chronicles living up to Paul's description? In what ways do they help meet your personal needs for both perseverance and encouragement?

_____

_____

For the group

You may want to focus your discussion for lesson 12 especially on some of the following issues, themes, and concepts (which are recognized as major overall themes in 1 and 2 Chronicles). Which of these are dealt with in some way in chapters 33–36, and how are they further developed there?

- The meaning and significance of God's covenant relationship with His people
- God's nature, especially as revealed by how He acts in the details of His people's history
- The importance and meaning of worship
- For God's people, the continuity of the present with the past
- The importance of obedience to God's Word and His laws, and our personal responsibility in that regard
- How sin brings disaster and judgment from God
- God's continued blessings and grace for His people
- The future hope of God's people
- The unity of God's people
- God's sovereignty over His people's lives and history

The following numbered questions in lesson 12 may stimulate your best and most helpful discussion: 1, 2, 8, 10, 12, 13, 14, and 15.

Allow enough discussion time to look back together and review all of 1 and 2 Chronicles as a whole. You can use the numbered questions 16–21 in this lesson to help you do that.

Once more, look also at the question in the margin under the heading "For Thought and Discussion."

1. Andrew E. Hill, *1 & 2 Chronicles*, The NIV Application Commentary series, ed. Terry Much (Grand Rapids, MI: Zondervan, 2003), 615.

2. Hill, 615–616.
3. Hill, 621.
4. Hill, 622.
5. Hill, 623.
6. Hill, 651–652.

STUDY AIDS

For further information on the material in this study, consider the following sources. They are available on the Internet (www.christianbook.com, www.amazon.com, etc.), or your local Christian bookstore should be able to order any of them if it does not carry them. Most seminary libraries have them, as well as many university and public libraries. If they are out of print, you might be able to find them online.

Commentaries on 1 and 2 Chronicles

Braun, Roddy L., and Raymond B. Dillard, *1 Chronicles, 2 Chronicles*, Word Biblical Commentary (Word, 1986, 1987).

Hill, Andrew E., *1 & 2 Chronicles*, NIV Application Commentary (Zondervan, 2003).

Japhet, Sara, *1 & 2 Chronicles*, Old Testament Library (Westminster John Knox, 1993).

Payne, J. Barton, *1, 2 Chronicles*, Expositor's Bible Commentary (Zondervan, 1988).

Pratt, Richard L., *1 & 2 Chronicles* (Mentor, 1998).

Selman, M. J., *1 Chronicles* and *2 Chronicles*, Tyndale Old Testament Commentaries (InterVarsity, 1994).

Historical background sources and handbooks

Bible study becomes more meaningful when modern Western readers understand the times and places in which the biblical authors lived. *The IVP Bible Background Commentary: Old Testament,* by John H. Walton, Victor H. Matthews, and Mark Chavalas (InterVarsity, 2000), provides insight into the ancient Near Eastern world, including its peoples, customs, and geography, to help contemporary readers better understand the context in which the Old Testament Scriptures were written.

A **handbook** of biblical customs can also be useful. Some good ones are the time-proven, updated classic *Halley's Bible Handbook with the New International Version,* by Henry H. Halley (Zondervan, 2007), and the inexpensive paperback *Manners and Customs in the Bible,* by Victor H. Matthews (Hendrickson, 1991).

Concordances, dictionaries, and encyclopedias

A **concordance** lists words of the Bible alphabetically along with each verse in which the word appears. It lets you do your own word studies. An *exhaustive* concordance lists every word used in a given translation, while an *abridged* or *complete* concordance omits either some words, some occurrences of the word, or both.

Two of the best exhaustive concordances are *Strong's Exhaustive Concordance* and *The Strongest NIV Exhaustive Concordance. Strong's* is available based on the King James Version of the Bible and the New American Standard Bible. *Strong's* has an index by which you can find out which Greek or Hebrew word is used in a given English verse. The NIV concordance does the same thing except it also includes an index for Aramaic words in the original texts from which the NIV was translated. However, neither concordance requires knowledge of the original languages. *Strong's* is available online at www.biblestudytools.com. Both are also available in hard copy.

A **Bible dictionary** or **Bible encyclopedia** alphabetically lists articles about people, places, doctrines, important words, customs, and geography of the Bible.

Holman Illustrated Bible Dictionary, by C. Brand, C. W. Draper, and A. England (B&H, 2003), offers more than seven hundred color photos, illustrations, and charts; sixty full-color maps; and up-to-date archeological findings, along with exhaustive definitions of people, places, things, and events—dealing with every subject in the Bible. It uses a variety of Bible translations and is the only dictionary that includes the HCSB, NIV, KJV, RSV, NRSV, REB, NASB, ESV, and TEV.

The New Unger's Bible Dictionary, Revised and Expanded, by Merrill F. Unger (Moody, 2006), has been a best seller for almost fifty years. Its 6,700-plus entries reflect the most current scholarship and more than 1,200,000 words are supplemented with detailed essays, colorful photography and maps, and dozens of charts and illustrations to enhance your understanding of God's Word. Based on the New American Standard Version.

The Zondervan Encyclopedia of the Bible, edited by Moisés Silva and Merrill C. Tenney (Zondervan, 2008), is excellent and exhaustive. However, its five 1,000-page volumes are a financial investment, so all but very serious students may prefer to use it at a church, public college, or seminary library.

Unlike a Bible dictionary in the above sense, *Vine's Complete Expository Dictionary of Old and New Testament Words,* by W. E. Vine, Merrill F. Unger, and William White Jr. (Thomas Nelson, 1996), alphabetically lists major words used in the King James Version and defines each Old Testament Hebrew or New Testament Greek word the KJV translates with that English word. *Vine's* lists verse references where that Hebrew or Greek word appears so that you can do your own cross-references and word studies without knowing the original languages.

The Brown-Driver-Briggs Hebrew and English Lexicon, by Francis Brown, C. Briggs, and S. R. Driver (Hendrickson, 1996), is probably the most respected and comprehensive Bible lexicon for Old Testament studies. *BDB* gives not only dictionary definitions for each word but relates each word to its Old Testament usage and categorizes its nuances of meaning.

Bible atlases and map books

A **Bible atlas** can be a great aid to understanding what is going on in a book of the Bible and how geography affected events. Here are a few good choices:

The Hammond Atlas of Bible Lands (Langenscheidt, 2007) packs a ton of resources into just sixty-four pages. Maps, of course, but also photographs, illustrations, and a comprehensive timeline. Includes an introduction to the unique geography of the Holy Land, including terrain, trade routes, vegetation, and climate information.

The New Moody Atlas of the Bible, by Barry J. Beitzel (Moody, 2009), is scholarly, very evangelical, and full of theological text, indexes, and references. Beitzel shows vividly how God prepared the land of Israel perfectly for the acts of salvation He was going to accomplish in it.

Then and Now Bible Maps Insert (Rose, 2008) is a nifty paperback that is sized just right to fit inside your Bible cover. Only forty-four pages long, it features clear plastic overlays of modern-day cities and countries so you can see what nation or city now occupies the Bible setting you are reading about. Every major city of the Bible is included.

For small-group leaders

Discipleship Journal's Best Small-Group Ideas, Volumes 1 and 2 (NavPress, 2005). Each volume is packed with 101 of the best hands-on tips and group-building principles from *Discipleship Journal's* "Small Group Letter" and "DJ Plus" as well as articles from the magazine. They will help you inject new passion into the life of your small group.

Donahue, Bill. *Leading Life-Changing Small Groups* (Zondervan, 2002). This comprehensive resource is packed with information, practical tips, and insights that will teach you about small-group philosophy and structure, discipleship, conducting meetings, and more.

McBride, Neal F. *How to Build a Small-Groups Ministry* (NavPress, 1994). *How to Build a Small-Groups Ministry* is a time-proven, hands-on workbook for pastors and lay leaders that includes everything you need to know to develop a plan that fits your unique church. Through basic principles, case studies, and worksheets, McBride leads you through twelve logical steps for organizing and administering a small-groups ministry.

McBride, Neal F. *How to Lead Small Groups* (NavPress, 1990). This book covers leadership skills for all kinds of small groups: Bible study, fellowship, task, and support groups. Filled with step-by-step guidance and practical exercises to help you grasp the critical aspects of small-group leadership and dynamics.

Miller, Tara, and Jenn Peppers. *Finding the Flow: A Guide for Leading Small Groups and Gatherings* (IVP Connect, 2008). *Finding the Flow* offers a fresh take on leading small groups by seeking to develop the leader's small-group facilitation skills.

Bible study methods

Discipleship Journal's Best Bible Study Methods (NavPress, 2002). This is a collection of thirty-two creative ways to explore Scripture that will help you enjoy studying God's Word more.

Hendricks, Howard, and William Hendricks. *Living by the Book: The Art and Science of Reading the Bible* (Moody, 2007). *Living by the Book* offers a practical three-step process that will help you master simple yet effective inductive methods of observation, interpretation, and application that will make all the difference in your time with God's Word. A workbook by the same title is also available to go along with the book.

The Navigator Bible Studies Handbook (NavPress, 1994). This resource teaches the underlying principles for doing good inductive Bible study, including instructions on doing queston-and-answer studies, verse-analysis studies, chapter-analysis studies, and topical studies.

Warren, Rick. *Rick Warren's Bible Study Methods: Twelve Ways You Can Unlock God's Word* (HarperCollins, 2006). Rick Warren offers simple, step-by-step instructions, guiding you through twelve different approaches to studying the Bible for yourself with the goal of becoming more like Jesus.